I0605377

Also by Ross W. Greene, PhD

The Explosive Child: A New Approach for Understanding and Parenting Easily Frustrated, Chronically Inflexible Children

Lost at School: Why Our Kids with Behavioral Challenges Are Falling Through the Cracks and How We Can Help Them

Lost and Found: Helping Behaviorally Challenging Students (and While You're At It, All the Others)

Raising Human Beings: Creating a Collaborative Partnership with Your Child

THE KIDS WHO AREN'T OKAY

The Urgent Case for Reimagining Support, Belonging, and Hope in Schools

Ross W. Greene, PhD

with Cynthia Graton and Ryan Gleason

SCRIBNER

New York Amsterdam/Antwerp London
Toronto Sydney/Melbourne New Delhi

Scribner
An Imprint of Simon & Schuster, LLC
1230 Avenue of the Americas
New York, NY 10020

First Scribner hardcover edition February 2026

Interior design by Silverglass

Manufactured in the United States of America

3 5 7 9 10 8 6 4 2

Library of Congress Cataloging-in-Publication Data is available.

ISBN 978-1-6682-0390-3
ISBN 978-1-6682-0397-2 (ebook)

"We cannot solve problems with the same thinking that created them."

—Albert Einstein

"Mā te rongo, ka mōhio . . . Mā te mōhio, ka Mārama."
(From listening comes knowledge . . . From knowledge comes understanding)

—Māori proverb

"We are where we are, however we got here. What matters is where we go next."

—Isaac Marion

Contents

Introduction

The numbers are alarming. Very high rates of anxiety and depression in adolescents, especially among (but not limited to) girls, and higher in the U.S. than in other countries. Sharply escalating rates of concerning behaviors at school, especially among (but not limited to) boys. Growing rates of suicide and suicide attempts among adolescents. Higher than ever rates of chronic school absenteeism (the national average in the U.S. is currently 23 percent). These trends were in motion before the pandemic. And they tell us all is not well.

Of course, COVID didn't help. Many students lost two to three years of academic and social learning during the pandemic. And students weren't the only ones to suffer; the demands placed on educators and parents were remarkably intense. Then came the rush back to normal, something for which many students and educators simply weren't ready. Not after what they'd all been through. Rates of teacher and principal attrition spiked during and immediately following the pandemic, and most of those positions are still not filled five years later, leaving many schools and school systems massively short-staffed.

Pandemic aside, schools are now bearing the weight of all the pressures and politics of society. It seems that everyone is aggrieved these days, and some of those grievances relate to school. Some parents and educators are livid about various aspects of the curriculum and what they consider to be lax discipline. Other parents and educators are irate that the use of punitive, exclusionary disciplinary practices is still so commonplace, having seen the harm caused to many students by such practices. Parents who feel that the individual differences of their kids are not being honored and respected at school are particularly aggrieved. Educators are aggrieved about pay, high-stakes testing, safety, and the expectation that they be all things to all students.

And there are a ton of developments that have occurred over the past twenty or so years that have made it way harder to be a kid, and a lot of those developments relate to schools. The short list (you'll read the long one in chapter 1) includes high-stakes testing (gauging the performance of a school, principal, or teacher based on test scores was a bad idea from the get-go), school shootings (there have been over 400 in the U.S. since Columbine in April 1999—a number that doesn't include colleges and universities—which is a major source of anxiety for students *and* educators *and* parents), zero tolerance policies (which made schools ever-more rigid and unforgiving but no safer), and an unrelenting emphasis on punitive, exclusionary discipline (over 600,000 in-school and out-of-school suspensions annually in the U.S., nearly 100,000 expulsions annually, 70,000 yearly instances of corporal punishment, and 70,000 annual instances of restraint and seclusion).

So, with all these forces making life harder, and with the statistics telling us that all is not well, a lot of folks are asking the question, *Are the kids okay?*

Very surprisingly, many still are. Not surprisingly, many more than ever aren't. This book is about both groups, but it's mostly focused on the ones who aren't. The ones who are most vulnerable when we don't get it right, the students with any variety of special needs; academic, social, and behavioral differences; and socioeconomic disadvantages. The fact that their numbers are growing tells us the countless hours of meetings, extra resources, and planning that occur in schools to help them haven't been enough, and that we can't keep doing things the same way.

In the ensuing pages, I and my co-authors—Cynthia Graton and Ryan Gleason—describe what's not working for those kids and why. Fair warning: some tried-and-true, long-standing practices aren't working. And we're going to describe how to change those things. The changes we recommend benefit vulnerable students the most, but they also benefit all students, along with their educators and parents. The ideas we propose have already been implemented by many (but nowhere nearly enough) schools. Yet many educators have never been exposed to them.

No time like the present.

As it relates to what we can do about the current scenario, schools have some reimagining to do. Schools are still largely oriented toward students who *are* doing well and hope that the various supports and services provided to the kids who *aren't* doing will see them through. Sometimes that works; often it doesn't (which explains why so many kids still aren't doing well). What if, with so many students struggling, we flipped the script? What if we were oriented toward creating learning environments that work for the students who *aren't* doing well? They would do better, but so would the kids who are currently doing well. There's a lot of developmental variability walking through that door. We need to be responsive to it.

This seems like a good time to be clear about the definition of good teaching: *meeting every student where they're at*. We'll explore that definition further in the ensuing pages. But it doesn't mean letting kids do whatever they want or lowering standards. For now, let's just state what is supposedly obvious: You're going to get a lot more out of a student if you meet them where they're at than if you don't.

We also need to stop being late. A lot of the practices school systems have been training educators to apply to our most vulnerable kids are reactive—that is, they occur *after* those students become agitated or escalated. School systems spend hundreds of millions of dollars every year training educators on de-escalation techniques, calming corners, how to use blocking pads, restraint . . . and they're all late. Crisis *management* practices don't help students, or their classmates, or educators. This book provides a technology for being *early*.

And we need to stop being so unilateral. You've already read about the numbers of punitive, exclusionary disciplinary practices used in American schools every year. Those practices are most often applied to our most vulnerable students, time after time. This book provides a technology for *collaborating* with kids, involving them in the process of solving the problems that are causing their concerning behaviors. Being unilateral hasn't worked for our most vulnerable students and won't. Finding out what's been making it hard for students to meet expectations and working together toward solutions does work.

Interestingly, a lot of the policies, structures, assessment practices, paperwork, and schedules in schools push us away from meeting kids where they're at and toward being late and unilateral. That's a big part of why educators feel they have no time to do much of anything besides the academic curriculum. If you're an educator, you inherited a lot of those structures. But just because you inherited them doesn't mean you can't change them.

There are lots of resources out there for how to improve schools. There is no profession that has more ideas thrown at (and sold to) it than educators. As a result, many educators have a bad case of initiative fatigue. But the ideas you'll be reading in this book are worthy of your attention, your energy, and your commitment. Unlike many other initiatives, the practices described in this book are evidence-based. Schools that implement these practices dramatically reduce concerning behaviors, are safer, reduce (or eliminate) restraint, seclusion, discipline referrals, and other punitive, exclusionary disciplinary practices, and save time. They also save a lot of kids.

So, you're about to embark on a journey. A journey that is likely to challenge existing beliefs, cause you to question existing practices, and make you wonder why things have been the way they've been for so long. All good.

There are descriptions of some students and educators in the ensuing chapters. Except for those in chapter 8, these descriptions are meant to be illustrative and do not describe specific individuals. Anxiety, depression, behavioral challenges, suicidality, and chronic school absenteeism are all frustration or distress responses. For ease of exposition, in this book we use the term *concerning behavior* to encompass these different responses.

This seems like a good time to introduce you to my amazing coauthors, Ryan Gleason and Cynthia Graton. Ryan has been principal at Yarmouth (Maine) Elementary School since 2017 and was recognized as Maine's 2022 National Distinguished Principal. Ryan was previously assistant principal at Durham (Maine) Community School and assistant principal at Falmouth (Maine) Elementary School, and has implemented the Collaborative & Proactive Solutions in all the schools in which he has held a leadership position. Cynthia is a psychoeducator based in Montreal and the director of training at Lives in the Balance. She has over twenty-five years of experience working with children and adolescents with complex behavioral challenges and has overseen large-scale implementation of the CPS model in schools, clinics, and youth-serving systems around the world.

1

What's the Matter with Kids Today?

This is a question that adults have been asking about younger generations since way before *Bye Bye Birdie* brought it into our consciousness. And yet, if you read the Introduction—or, better yet, you're an educator or parent—you know that there may be something to it this time. But now it's not the character of the younger generation we're contemplating, it's their mental health, with many indicators—escalated rates of anxiety, depression, suicidality, chronic school absenteeism, and concerning behavior—suggesting that, while most kids are still doing OK, more kids than ever aren't doing very well at all.

It's not like kids have ever gotten off easy. Back in the good old days—when they were on the hook for foraging or hunting for food, generating income, or working the farm—kids worried about things like death (their own and that of family members) due to wild beasts, wars, outbreaks of violence, diseases, natural calamities, and during childbirth (all still threats, just not quite to the same degree); food and housing insecurity (still issues for many, just not as many); harsh discipline (also still an issue for many); and whatever fears religions and superstitions instilled. Back then, most adults weren't particularly concerned about how the kids were doing or about the importance of nurturing, protecting, and educating them. Adults didn't really start thinking about those things until the past two centuries.

It was in the 1900s that we started *studying* children. We began identifying phases of development, started bifurcating typical and atypical development, and eventually assembled a wide array of childhood psychiatric disorders to demarcate specific categories of concerning behaviors (a list that continues to expand). We created instruments for quantifying children's intelligence and levels of academic skills, anxiety, depression, social skills, and concerning behavior. We started training professionals who specialized in treating the psychological difficulties of childhood, heavily influenced by smart people like Sigmund Freud and B. F. Skinner. In 1989, the United Nations Convention on the Rights of the Child recognized children as individuals with rights. Apparently, this included the right to be treated with psychotropic medication—something that became commonplace in the 1990s—especially if a child had trouble focusing, sitting still, controlling their impulses, regulating their emotions, or was overly anxious or depressed.

Over the past twenty years, thanks to a flood of increasingly accessible information, kids have become much more aware of global events, social issues, and crises, and much earlier in life. Kids are often exposed to content that bypasses the traditional trajectory of childhood and that they may not have the maturity or support to process. Children's shows and books today often cover themes of racism, inequality, gender identity, and environmental crisis that would have been avoided or sanitized in the past. Topics like mental health, identity, injustice, and violence are now often part of school curricula. The upside is that many kids are more socially conscious and emotionally intelligent and are better prepared to navigate a complex world. The downside is that increased awareness of the bad stuff can lead to empathy fatigue and, especially in those most vulnerable, increased mental health concerns.

A deeper dive on these factors is coming up next. But let's first establish that intermittent anxiety, depression, disengagement, and concerning behavior are part of the human experience. In general, they tell us that a human being is in distress. When anxiety, depression, concerning behavior, and disengagement are more persistent and severe—especially compared to individuals of the same age or gender—we know that a human being is in more persistent and severe distress (and more likely to meet diagnostic criteria for a psychiatric disorder). We also know that, due to a mix of a wide variety of environmental and genetic factors, some human beings (kids included) are more vulnerable to stress than others. This explains why two human beings exposed to the exact same stressor might respond in completely different ways. But no matter how well-equipped an individual might be, their capacity to handle stress can be compromised if the sheer intensity, quantity, and persistence of stressors exceeds their capacity to cope. Finally, and this is important, we know that protective factors—such as supportive, stable, nurturing environments—can buffer against the impact of stress.

So, when we see dramatically more kids exhibiting anxiety, depression, concerning behavior, suicidality, and school absenteeism, it tells us that we need to take a hard look at the ecosystems in which they exist and start asking some questions. What factors have made it harder and more stressful to be a kid? Which kids are most adversely affected by those factors? Those are the questions we'll be focused on in the rest of this chapter. Then we'll turn our attention to two others: As regards the ecosystem that is the focal point of this book, what can educators and schools do to support the most vulnerable kids and buffer against the impact of those factors? And are there practices and structures in schools that make it harder for educators to do that?

The factors delineated below aren't intended to be exhaustive and aren't really in any particular order.

The Columbine High School Massacre

We're going to start with the Columbine tragedy, which shocked the national consciousness in April 1999. Little did we know the carnage and heartbreak that was to come in the ensuing twenty-six years. The vice president of the United States declared in 2025 that school shootings have become a *fact of life*. Whether that's a political hedge, since those shootings are now occurring on his watch and that of his boss, or an acknowledgment that we don't have the political will to do anything about them, it's still sending a powerful message to kids and educators about the degree to which we value their lives. The politicians who have been sitting on their hands on this issue have blood on those hands. They've also signed kids and educators up for a lot of anxiety and depression. Well over 50 percent of kids between the ages of thirteen and twenty-one report experiencing fear, stress, anxiety, and depression over the prospect of being shot at school, with about one-fourth reporting that their anxiety is significant. Unsurprisingly, the percentages are strikingly similar for educators. In the aggregate, younger kids seem to be somewhat less anxious about school shootings, but are not invulnerable to stress from media coverage of school shootings and active-shooter drills.

Aside from age, factors that have also been shown to heighten the likelihood of anxiety about school shootings in kids include gender (in the aggregate, girls are more anxious about them than boys), ethnicity (students of color often report higher levels of concern about school shootings, sometimes because of exposure to neighborhood violence), and students with existing mental health difficulties (students predisposed to anxiety and depression are more vulnerable to heightened fear responses).

As a sidenote, for those who believe that having a police officer in every school is the answer, the scant research on whether school resource officers (SROs) make schools safer is equivocal. By contrast, the research is not equivocal on whether the presence of SROs increases arrests for minor infractions that occur in schools. Nor is the research equivocal on the students who are disproportionately arrested for those minor infractions (black and brown children and/or those with disabilities). And having SROs in schools certainly hasn't made a dent in rates of anxiety and depression in kids.

High-Stakes Testing

It was also in the late 1990s that high-stakes testing became the norm in the United States. The goals were admirable: better education, equity, and holding schools and teachers accountable for student outcomes. The results have been spectacularly underwhelming. Among other unfavorable outcomes, the repercussions of poor performance on high-stakes tests—grade retention, poor teacher evaluations, being identified as a failing school—have contributed to significant stress in both students and educators. Many educators have cited testing pressure and resulting demoralization as a cause for leaving the profession. We've heard many educators comment that high-stakes testing took all the humanity out of their jobs. Given that we've always relied on educators to be among the most important socialization agents in our society, that can't be good. Not for kids and not for educator retention and job satisfaction. And while standards are fine and it is true that every kid can learn, the risk of raising the bar higher is that more kids will have difficulty meeting expectations.

Which students have suffered the most from the high-stakes testing scenario? Not surprisingly, low-income students have suffered disproportionately, because schools in low-income communities had to double-down on test prep in response to accountability mandates and students in underperforming schools were more likely to be retained, tracked into low-level classes, or have their schools closed. Students with disabilities have suffered as well, because one-size-fits-all testing often ignored the needs and accommodations required for students with Individualized Education Plans (IEPs) and education accommodation plans (504 Plans), and because many were expected to take grade-level standardized tests without appropriate modifications. English Language Learners (who were often tested in English before they had full English proficiency) and young students (because developmentally inappropriate pressure can interfere with love of learning during critical formative years) were also adversely affected.

Zero Tolerance Policies

Largely as a response to Columbine, schools throughout the U.S. decided that the best way to keep schools safe was to apply zero tolerance policies, mandating strict, predetermined punishments (like suspension or expulsion) for certain behaviors, including relatively minor infractions. While it might be instinctive, for some anyway, to take a hard line in the midst of a crisis, the data on zero tolerance policies are compelling: they made things worse (evidence for the maxim that for every problem there is a solution that is simple, neat, and wrong). These policies increased suspensions and expulsions, leading to lost learning time; had a disproportionately negative effect on marginalized students; and eroded trust between students and adults, making schools feel less supportive. Schools became more punitive, with a stronger emphasis on control and compliance rather than relationship-building and problem-solving. Teachers often felt compelled to enforce harsh punishments even when inappropriate, straining relationships with students and families.

Insufficient Mental Health Services for Kids

There are insufficient mental health resources to meet the increasing demand. The U.S. has a critical shortage of child and adolescent psychiatrists, psychiatric nurses, and other mental health providers. The lack of access to mental health care is especially acute in low-income families, as they are more likely to rely on Medicaid, which isn't accepted by many private providers due to administrative burdens and low payment. Rural areas and low-income urban neighborhoods often have few or no licensed mental health professionals for children and teens, and community mental health centers that serve disadvantaged populations are often underfunded and face unstable staffing and high caseloads.

Starting in the 1960s, the U.S. began closing large psychiatric hospitals, including those serving youth. While the plan was to replace them with community-based mental health care, funding and infrastructure for those services didn't keep pace. As a result, the number of inpatient psychiatric beds for children steadily declined, even as mental health needs increased. In many states, there are fewer than 10 pediatric psychiatric beds per 100,000 children, and some large regions have no inpatient psychiatric beds for children at all. Children with complex needs, public insurance, or concerning behaviors are often turned away or placed on long waiting lists. Kids sometimes wait days, weeks, or *months* in emergency rooms because there's nowhere else for them to go. Inpatient stays sometimes don't accomplish much—the length-of-stays are often too brief—but at least kids are, theoretically, safe while they're on a unit and fresh eyes and expertise can sometimes foster better aftercare.

Being Neurodivergent

Neurodivergent means that a person's brain functions or processes in ways that diverge from what is considered "typical" or neurotypical. The term is often used to describe individuals whose cognitive or neurological development differs from the dominant societal norms, especially in areas like social skills, attention, learning, communication, and sensory processing, and therefore can include kids diagnosed with any variety of psychiatric disorders and profiles, including autism, pathological demand avoidance (PDA), attention-deficit hyperactivity disorder (ADHD), sensory processing disorders, Tourette's disorder, and a variety of learning difficulties in areas such as reading, writing, and math.

Neurodivergence challenges the notion that there's only one "correct" way for a brain to function. The Neurodivergent Paradigm views variations in functioning as part of natural human diversity, not as something inherently wrong or broken. Indeed, the neurodivergent community has grown weary of being told they're *not* OK. Being a neurodivergent child can come with unique strengths, but it also comes with the challenges of navigating a world that isn't designed with developmental variability in mind. The challenges don't necessarily stem from the neurodivergence itself, but rather from how society—including schools—responds to it.

For example, neurodivergent children are often misunderstood by adults and peers who misinterpret their behavior as disobedience or lack of effort. Most classrooms are designed for neuromajority learners, and not all schools offer accommodations (like extended time, sensory breaks, or alternate learning formats). Some children are underestimated (especially if they're nonspeaking or have intellectual disabilities), while others are assumed to be able in some areas because they're able in others. Neurodivergent children may struggle with social cues, impulse control, or emotional regulation, leading to social exclusion or bullying. When overwhelmed, some neurodivergent children may lose the ability to function in the moment, which is often misinterpreted as willful, intentional misbehavior. Many neurodivergent kids learn to "mask" their differences to avoid negative attention, which can be emotionally exhausting and harmful to their sense of identity. When these differences aren't well-understood and supported, the disadvantages can be profound.

Being a Boy

There's been much written about why it's harder to be a boy these days. Boys, on average, score lower in reading and writing than girls in many countries. They are also more likely to be diagnosed with ADHD, oppositional defiant disorder (ODD), conduct disorder (CD), learning difficulties, and to drop out of school. Schools often emphasize behavior, organization, and verbal communication, skills that many boys (especially early in development) struggle with compared to girls. In many places, significantly fewer boys than girls go to and graduate from college. This shift has reversed what used to be a male-dominated higher education system. The decline in manufacturing and blue-collar jobs (which historically employed many men) has hit boys in working-class communities especially hard. In a job market that increasingly favors communication, collaboration, and caregiving skills, boys can be at a disadvantage. Boys are still often discouraged from expressing vulnerability or emotions, which can lead to stress and isolation. Boys are often told to be strong, but also sensitive. To lead but also yield. There's often little guidance on how to navigate this balance. And, especially in single-parent households, many boys are growing up in the absence of consistent male mentors.

Being a Girl

Much has also been written about why it's harder to be a girl these days. In general, girls have higher rates of anxiety and depression than boys. But girls are also exposed to constant, often unrealistic beauty standards and popularity metrics. Girls often feel they must excel academically, socially, and physically, creating enormous internal pressure. Girls are socialized to maintain a hard-to-achieve balance between being smart, kind, pretty, and assertive but not aggressive. There are often conflicting messages: be empowered, but not too much; be natural but also look perfect; be independent but not intimidating. Many girls grow up having to think constantly about their safety in public and private spaces. Harassment, stalking, and assault are real and common fears. And in a victim-blaming culture, girls are too often made to feel responsible for their own victimization.

Being LGBTQ+

Being an LGBTQ+ youth today can come with significant challenges, even as society has become more open in some areas. For many young people, figuring out their sexual orientation or gender identity is a deeply personal and sometimes difficult process, and it's made harder when they face rejection, discrimination, disapproval, or lack of understanding. Coming out can lead to conflict, hostility, or even being kicked out of the home (LGBTQ+ youth are overrepresented among homeless youth in the U.S.). Some LGBTQ+ youth grow up in communities where their sexual or gender identity is considered sinful, shameful, or unnatural, and LGBTQ+ students often face verbal harassment, social exclusion, and sometimes physical threats at school. Trans and nonbinary students are especially targeted. Social media can be a double-edged sword, providing connection but also exposing youth to cyberbullying, hate, and harmful content. Many live with anxiety that someone will reveal their identity without their consent.

LGBTQ+ youth face disproportionately high rates of mental health challenges due to the stress of stigma, isolation, or rejection. LGBTQ+ youth—especially trans youth—are at much higher risk of suicidal thoughts and attempts than their non-LGBTQ+ peers. In many states, laws have been passed or proposed that ban discussion of LGBTQ+ topics in schools (e.g., "Don't Say Gay" laws), restrict access to gender-affirming care, or limit rights for trans youth. Trans youth are often denied the right to use the bathroom that matches their gender identity or to play on sports teams, increasing feelings of exclusion and danger. Books, curriculum, and Pride events are being challenged or banned in some schools and communities, which sends the message that their existence is controversial.

Being Black or Brown

While progress has been made in many areas, being a black or brown child in the U.S. today can still come with numerous systemic disadvantages rooted in long-standing racial inequalities. Schools in predominantly black and brown communities often receive less funding due to property tax–based education systems. Black and brown students are far more likely to face harsh disciplinary actions at school, such as corporal punishment, suspensions, and expulsions, starting as early as preschool. Biases among educators can result in lowered expectations, fewer referrals to gifted programs, and less academic encouragement. Black and brown children often encounter subtle (and sometimes overt) forms of racism from peers, teachers, or strangers. Structural barriers reduce access to high-quality healthcare, both physical and mental. Cultural stigma and lack of culturally competent care often result in untreated mental health issues. Black and brown children are more likely to live in poverty, which is linked to food insecurity, housing instability, and limited educational opportunities. The racial wealth gap limits access to resources, extracurriculars, and generational advantages.

Being White

It is true that many white children in the U.S. benefit from systemic advantages in areas like education, policing, and economic opportunity due to long-standing social and institutional structures, but it is also true that many don't. White children who live in poverty suffer the same difficulties as children of other ethnicities who live in poverty, including addiction in the family, housing insecurity, and lack of opportunity. As noted above, economic shifts of the past two to three decades, especially in rural and postindustrial areas, have adversely affected many white working-class communities. As the U.S. becomes more racially and ethnically diverse, some white kids (and their parents) interpret these disadvantages and shifts as being due to a perceived loss of status and cultural dominance. Some blame immigration or affirmative action for their declining fortunes, rather than automation or globalization. Many white Americans may feel overlooked by diversity-focused narratives or programs, and some white people feel alienated by progressive rhetoric that focuses on racial injustice, interpreting it as blaming or marginalizing them. Some view diversity programs as taking away opportunities from white people, especially in college admissions or hiring. Disconnected or isolated white youth—particularly boys—may be more easily targeted by extremist or white supremacist content online that preys on insecurity or resentment. And white children, especially boys, may feel their emotional or psychological struggles are dismissed because they're assumed to be privileged in all aspects.

Reduced Influence of Religion

The influence and popularity of religion began declining in the U.S. in the 1990s, with the most dramatic drop occurring since the early 2000s, particularly among younger generations. While there are different views on whether that's a positive development, those who are no longer relying on religion as a guiding force in many aspects of life are now going solo (or relying on other influences) to figure things out on their own. And, as noted above, the figuring out starts earlier than ever.

For example, over the past two decades, kids in the U.S. and in many parts of the world have been exploring and expressing more fluid ideas related to sexuality. That people are now freer to express their sexual identity and somewhat less likely to experience intolerance, stigma, shame, and discrimination is viewed by many as a positive development. And studies have shown that LGBTQ+ youth who are supported early in their identity development have lower rates of depression and suicide. But confusion, anxiety, and depression can follow when such exploration occurs before kids are developmentally ready. When are they developmentally ready? As with most things, it's different for different kids.

Gender roles are another realm that was previously governed by religion or traditional social codes. Back when Ward and June Cleaver were showing us how it's done, Ward was the breadwinner, had a stable job, and was unlikely to be uprooted to another city. June took care of the house and the kids. Pretty straightforward stuff. Now there are lots of Junes in the workplace and lots of Wards staying home with the kids. Stereotypes are out. Which means we're all on the hook for figuring out what feels right.

Better? That depends on your point of view. But certainly, at least in some ways, harder.

Home and Family Life

Beginning in the 1980s and 1990s, families had to rely on a second income to maintain the standard of living that was previously possible with one income (housing, education, and healthcare costs had begun to outpace wage growth). Thus, more women joined the workforce, not only because of equality but out of economic necessity. In many families, kids are getting less of both of their parents. While research tells us that the effects on kids of time spent with parents is more a matter of quality rather than quantity, for some parents, the stress of juggling work, family, and money has contributed to conflict, burnout, and reduced emotional support for kids. Lack of parental supervision after school has brought "latchkey kids" into our consciousness, and these kids often show increased risk-taking, lower academic performance, and behavior problems.

Caregiver Mental Health

We can't examine children's mental health outside the context of the mental health of their caregivers. Along those lines, multiple national studies and health advisories show that mental health among parents in the U.S. has declined significantly since before COVID, with ongoing elevated stress, anxiety, and depression. Family studies have shown that rates of parental depression doubled post-pandemic. Parental stress and mental health challenges are strongly correlated with poor child outcomes.

Educator mental health in the U.S. has declined significantly since pre-COVID as well. The pandemic intensified existing chronic stress and created new pressures, resulting in higher levels of anxiety, depression, burnout, and heightened intentions to leave the profession. Before COVID, educator mental health was already strained by burnout and reformation fatigue. During COVID, rates of anxiety and depression spiked dramatically. Post-COVID, symptoms have persisted and worsened, fueled by systemic issues: excessive demands, diminished support structures, and a struggling school environment. In the U.S., teachers report worsening working conditions post-pandemic, with declines in teacher safety, classroom climate, trust in leadership, and overall job quality from 2021 to 2023. As alluded to earlier, rising job demands, reduced autonomy, and increased behavioral issues among students are cited as key stress drivers.

Changing Definitions of Success

In the 1950s, success was defined by a stable job, marriage, homeownership, and a family. Upward mobility through hard work was the way things were done. Again, pretty straightforward stuff, especially for middle-class white people. After a twenty-year sojourn into civil rights and feminism in the 1970s and 1980s—punctuated by the Vietnam War—the 1990s saw success defined by academic performance, elite college admissions, and extracurricular overload. In that hypercompetitive culture, another new term—"helicopter parenting"—was added to our vocabularies. Even kindergartens are increasingly focused on literacy and numeracy at the expense of play-based learning. For many kids, childhood has become a performance treadmill, in sports, grades, and extracurriculars. The system rewards achievement, not development. The result is stress, burnout, and little time for joy or exploration.

With so many stressed-out kids, the definition of success in the last fifteen years was broadened to include emotional well-being, prompting the addition of social-emotional learning (SEL) curriculums to school life. Those programs enjoyed relatively brief half-lives; in many locations in the U.S., those curricula have now been banned or discontinued, due to concerns about the values they are thought to promote.

Politics

American politics were designed to be adversarial, but the political environment of the past twenty years or so—cancel culture, polarization, paralysis on solving many important problems—has produced a level of incivility that, according to some, has not been seen since the Civil War. The depth, persistence, and all-consuming nature of today's partisan divide are relatively modern and uniquely intense. Everyone is aggrieved about something, and a lot of those grievances are long-standing (not to mention legitimate). Everyone wants their pain to be known and their voice to be heard, which is all good, but not if we're not listening to each other. The absence of role modeling in solving problems collaboratively and civilly is appalling.

Are there kids who are more adversely affected by this scenario? Apparently so. Children who belong to communities that are often the subject of political debate or hostility—such as immigrants, LGBTQ+ youth, racial or religious minorities—may experience heightened stress, fear, or discrimination. For example, in the former category, children may worry about deportation or family separation. LGBTQ+ youth may face exclusion, bullying, or reduced access to supportive resources in states with anti-trans or anti-LGBTQ+ legislation. And political rhetoric (and the not-so-dark corners of the internet) can fuel racial profiling or harassment in kids who are already marginalized.

In schools or neighborhoods where political tensions run high—especially when adults model divisiveness—children may experience bullying or social exclusion and anxiety about expressing themselves for fear of being ostracized. Children who are exposed only to fear-based messages without help interpreting them can develop a skewed understanding of the world, adopt rigid or hostile viewpoints, and feel disconnected from peers who think differently.

Social Media and Cell Phones

Yes, this is the hot one right now. And there's no question that social media can contribute to the decline in mental health of some kids, especially those who use it excessively. But as you've read in the preceding pages, if we only focus on social media we're going to miss a lot of contributing factors. And since the research on the effects of social media on kids is equivocal and mostly correlational, drawing causal conclusions is, at this point, both precarious and premature. That said, kids are being targeted in social media like never before. Quite clearly, capitalism, not healthy child development, is the driving force. That shouldn't be surprising in a capitalistic society, nor is it new. It's just that we've moved beyond selling sugary cereals (which adults were more able to oversee and control) to selling things that seem far worse for children's mental health and more difficult to oversee and control. According to the U.S. Centers for Disease Control, 95 percent of teens use social media, and over a third say they use it constantly.

Many platforms are designed to be addictive, with level systems, loot, infinite scrolls, and endless feeds making it hard to stop. There is concern that boys are being fed a constant stream of extreme content that can normalize aggressive, hypermasculine, and misogynistic behavior and warp expectations about sex. The majority of boys have been exposed to pornography by the age of eleven or twelve. In girls, unrealistic beauty standards found on social media can contribute to chronic dissatisfaction with their own appearance. Girls also more often face relational bullying, including gossip, exclusion, and humiliation. Both girls and boys often tie their self-worth to online engagement. We could go on, but you get the idea.

The level of violence in social media and video games is quite concerning as well. But violence is also pervasive in what we watch on television (and in what some kids see routinely in their communities), and that's been true since we began watching the brutality of the Vietnam War every night on the evening news. Some kids and other humans are traumatized by and/or quite anxious about the constant flood of violence. Some habituate to the flood of violence or become numb to it. An understandable response, but it's definitely not ideal for human beings to be detached from the costs and harms of violence.

And, even worse, some are fascinated by it. Of course, it's not just violence that kids are accessing in social media; it's hate, anger, and rage. These ingredients have always been part of the human experience to varying degrees, sometimes moderated by religion and politics. Whether social media *causes* anger, hate, and rage is debatable, but there's no question that it makes it more *accessible*. And human beings who are vulnerable or feel marginalized for one reason or another are particularly susceptible to being pulled into the toxicity.

The search for meaning, purpose, and belonging and establishing one's values and identity are the major tasks of adolescence. That search can take kids in myriad directions, both positive and destructive. Most kids still find their identity through family, religion, school, academics, sports, clubs, community organizations, music, perhaps even a mental health diagnosis, and can find support for their identity in social media. Those who don't find positive meaning are at risk for alienation and nihilism, the belief that life and societal norms have no meaning. They have the potential to gravitate to far less positive social media influences.

The banning of cell phones in schools has become a popular starting point for addressing the potential harms of social media and cell phone use. Such bans have occurred in many school systems and some entire states. While banning cell phones might help students be less distracted at school, it doesn't reduce accessibility to the toxicity that exists in some corners of the web. And it won't address the vast array of preceding factors that are making it harder to be a kid these days. Whether issuing mandates is the best approach—as opposed to involving kids in helping solve the problem—is worth considering. Mandates often don't tend to work very well. That's a theme we'll be considering on a variety of issues in the rest of the book.

......

If the foregoing has you wondering how *any* kid is doing OK these days, we get it. No wonder there is an urgent need for reimagining hope, belonging, and support in school. The good news is that, despite everything you've just read, most kids are still doing OK. Generation Alpha, as they're known, is not to be underestimated. They're smart, digital, discerning, self-aware, self-protective, take a lot of selfies, and grow up fast, and they are as skeptical of and dissatisfied with the way adults and political leaders are handling things as the generations that preceded them. Many also feel that the unsolved problems created or kicked down the road by those prior generations have been left for them to solve. Life is challenging, no doubt; many are managing. But as we also noted, many more than ever are not, due to any or many of the factors we delineated above.

If you're an educator, you may be thinking: "I can't change all of those things!" And you're right; you may not actually be able to do anything about *most* of them. While we don't wish to diminish their importance or sound obtuse, for educators many of the challenges we described above fall into the IIWII category (It Is What It Is). What you *can* do is create school and classroom ecosystems that are as supportive, inclusive, hopeful, stable, nurturing, safe, and responsive as they are academically rigorous and interesting. You have the kids in your building six hours a day, five days a week, nine months a year; you can do kids a lot of good in that time despite—or perhaps especially because of—what's going on outside the building. The kids who aren't OK are walking through that door no matter what. You might as well help them. And the ecosystems you create for the kids who aren't doing OK are also going to be better for the kids who are doing OK. And better for you too.

Speaking of you, we know that you get a charge out of seeing your students grow and be successful. We know that having a good relationship with your students matters to you. And we know that what you read in this book is going to give you both of those things.

Closer Look: Is This My Job?

Let's be honest: it's less rewarding to be an educator these days. You're underpaid, underappreciated, undersupported, and underfunded (and that's only getting worse), and may have a bad case of initiative fatigue. You may feel unsafe in your classroom. Which means that you may not be especially enthusiastic about yet another set of new ideas and practices. But with so many kids struggling to show up and keep up, we have to examine our practices. We have to be responsive to what's walking in the door.

You might be thinking: OK, I'm game, but I'm not trained as a mental health professional. True enough. The good news is that you don't need to be trained as a mental health professional to help most of the kids who are struggling. And mental health professionals and educators do share some common territory, in that they're both helping professions. Most therapists are pretty good at listening and trying to understand (and lots of people—including kids who are struggling—don't feel heard and often feel misunderstood). But mental health professionals aren't the only ones doing the listening; lots of educators listen to kids as well. Though it comes more naturally to some than others, listening isn't a supernatural skill. Anyone can be a good listener, with some commitment, intentionality, and a few strategies. Most therapists are invested in showing their clients that they care; if you're an educator, that's not foreign territory either. And many therapists help their clients work on problems that are affecting their lives; educators have been solving problems with their students since forever.

Now, it's true that there are some mental health practitioners who are primarily focused on modifying kids' behavior. For reasons you'll be reading about, we'd recommend against that. And there are certainly some therapists who do more talking and advice-giving than collaborating; we'd recommend against that too. Mental health professionals often have vast knowledge of psychiatric diagnoses; if you don't, that could be working in your favor. Some therapists spend a lot of time interpreting what kids (and adults) say to them, almost as if they can read minds (it's these therapists who are most often caricatured on TV); that's not going to be your best play. As you'll see, skilled helping usually involves far more listening and far less divining. And some mental health practitioners devote a lot of attention to historical and environmental factors that may be contributing to a kid's difficulties; we don't recommend that either. A lot of that information isn't *actionable*, so it's probably not worth all the attention.

Don't sell yourself short. You can have a tremendous impact on those kids even though you're not trained as a mental health professional and aren't fluent in psychiatric diagnoses. You have a critical role to play. Reading this book is a good start.

You might also be thinking that your job performance is primarily being measured by the academic performance of your students, so attending to their emotional well-being isn't in your best interests. On part of that we're going to disagree. While it's true that your job performance is being assessed based on the academic performance of your students—and that most of the continuing education and professional development you receive is about academics—we think that attending to the emotional well-being of your students is in both their and your best interests and is likely to enhance academic performance.

And, finally, you might be thinking about how little time you have, and how unrealistic it is to consider adding anything more to your plate. We'll have to do something about that. Plus, what you'll be reading in the following pages is going to save you time. Lots of it.

....

"We can't change the direction of the wind, but we can adjust our sails."

—Jimmy Dean

2

Meeting Every Student Where They're At

If we were tasked with the mission of creating school and classroom ecosystems that worked for the students who are struggling, what would they look like? Probably not the way most classrooms look now. Most schools and classrooms are structured around the kids who *aren't* struggling (either that, or there are just some kids who are going to do well pretty much no matter what). But what would we do differently if we structured things in the opposite direction? Safe in the belief that what works for those who are struggling also works for those who aren't (and knowing that the reverse is not true), what structures, belief systems, and practices would we change?

We'd Focus on Developmental Variability

Developmental variability refers to the natural differences or fluctuations in how individuals develop over time. It applies to all domains of functioning—cognitive/academic, emotional, physical, and social—and it's *guaranteed* to be walking into your school and classroom. Amazingly enough, it's a term we don't hear very often in educator training or in schools. And yet, it's your reality. We should embrace it. The good news is that developmental variability isn't something you need to change; it's something you need to focus on, be responsive to, and plan for with intentionality. The quality of a school is measured by the degree to which it is responsive to the developmental variability of its students. (By the way, a good synonym for developmental variability is *diversity*.)

We'd Redefine Good Teaching

If the goal is to be responsive to the developmental variability in our classrooms, then we would define good teaching as *meeting every student where they're at*. This definition is broad enough to encompass the pursuit of high (yet highly individualized) expectations, getting the most out of every student (with each student as their own reference point), and being important socialization agents. It's also a good way to define *equity* (as opposed to equality, which means treating every student the same). Pursuing equality would only make sense if every student were the same. Meeting kids where they're at doesn't mean you think they're incapable—it means you think they *are* capable—but you're not going to see that they're capable if you're not meeting them where they're at.

So long as we're defining terms, what's it called when we provide equal access to opportunities and resources for students who might otherwise be excluded or marginalized because of their developmental variabilities? That, of course, is called *inclusion*. While the concepts of diversity, equity, and inclusion have been leveraged in the political realm, schools have no choice but to embrace and attend to them. Especially if we want to help the students who are struggling, but also if we want to be responsive to the unique characteristics of *every* student.

Meeting every student where they're at is hard work. *Not* meeting every student where they're at is way harder. As we mentioned in chapter 1, thanks to high-stakes testing, educators are under intense pressure to ensure that every student meets the same standard by the end of the school year, with evaluations of job performance and job security often pegged to how well they accomplish the mission. While there are supports that are designed to help students who are struggling to meet expectations, those supports often don't get the job done. High-stakes testing, even with supports added, has made it *harder* for educators to meet students where they're at.

Another factor, a sensitive one, has also made it harder to meet our definition of good teaching. The racial reckoning that has intermittently gripped the U.S. for centuries has intensified calls for ensuring that black and brown students receive full access to educational opportunities, something denied them since . . . well, since pretty much forever. (The U.S. isn't alone in this scenario; black and brown students in other countries have suffered similar fates.) Recognizing that black and brown students are just as capable as their white counterparts is a step forward, though perhaps a particularly unfortunate example of the *better late than never* adage. But if that recognition is accompanied by placing expectations on students that they are currently unable to meet, that's two steps back. It could also be construed as a case of advancing well-intentioned principles at the expense of meeting kids where they're at. We've seen this practice cause the students who are struggling the most—irrespective of skin color—to blow out of classrooms, wander hallways, and stop showing up. When those things happen, those students are, most assuredly, not accessing their educational opportunities.

What we're circling around here is a concept we call *expectation management*. Simply translated, this means giving conscious, deliberate thought to whether the expectations we're placing on students are currently in range for them, *with each student as their own reference point*. We fervently believe that if educators were managing their *expectations* better—and given permission to do so—they'd be managing *behavior* a lot less. And they'd be suspending, expelling, hitting, de-escalating, restraining, and secluding a lot less too.

How do we know if an expectation is in range for a student? That's a judgment call. But we have a simple, imperfect algorithm that may help you out. If a student can sometimes meet an expectation, it's in range. If a student is currently never meeting an expectation, it's probably out of range for now. Not forever, for now.

Now, at this point, you might be thinking that special education is supposed to be the mechanism by which we take care of all that developmental variability and try to meet students where they're at. As we discuss later, if we're relying exclusively on special education for that, we're selling general education and the kids short and creating an unfortunate and counterproductive distinction between the kids who are and aren't meeting our expectations.

We'd Accurately Interpret Concerning Behavior

What happens when we place expectations on students that they're unable to reliably meet? They, like the rest of us, exhibit a *frustration response*. The synonym for frustration response is *concerning behavior*. (We'll be using those two terms interchangeably throughout the book.) Put differently, a good way to cause lots of frustration responses in a classroom is to place lots of expectations on students that they're having difficulty meeting.

As a sidenote, kids also have highly variable frustration responses. Some kids have milder frustration responses such as whining, pouting, sulking, withdrawing, and crying. We refer to these frustration responses as *lucky*, because they tend to elicit empathy, nurturance, and support from adults. Other kids have more powerful frustration responses, such as screaming, swearing, hitting, spitting, kicking, biting, throwing, destroying, and eloping. We refer to these frustration responses as *unlucky*, because they're less likely to elicit empathy, nurturance, and support from adults. Indeed, they often elicit the most punitive, exclusionary disciplinary practices our schools and society have to offer. In other words, it's the kids with unlucky frustration responses that we're busy de-escalating, restraining, secluding, expelling, suspending, and hitting.

What explains the variability in frustration responses? If we pay attention to the research that has accumulated over the past forty to fifty years on kids with concerning behaviors—and we definitely should—the answer is *skills*. Some students are blessed with the skills to handle problems and frustrations adaptively and others just aren't. We're referring here to global skills such as flexibility/adaptability, frustration tolerance, problem-solving, and emotion regulation (plus a whole bunch more you'll be reading about soon).

But whether lucky or unlucky, the most important thing to know about concerning behavior is that it *communicates* that there's an expectation a student is having difficulty reliably meeting.

Notice that last sentence didn't say anything about a student's level of motivation. That's because there isn't a single study—not one—telling us that unlucky frustration responses are due to poor motivation. That being the case, we are left to ponder why, for so long, the standard approach to handling concerning behavior in most schools has been to apply motivational strategies—consequences, some form of reward and/or punishment—aimed at ensuring that kids have the *incentive* to behave adaptively.

And why is the student having difficulty meeting an expectation in the first place? That's often also about skills, but in other domains such as reading, math, spelling, writing, starting conversations, entering groups, sharing, taking turns, and so forth.

Q & A

Question: Now, hold on a second. You're saying that poor motivation isn't what's going on when a student isn't meeting an expectation?

Answer: That's right.

Question: But that's what I was trained to believe!
Answer: That's how most of us were trained. That doesn't make it true. It may actually come as a bit of a relief to know that you're no longer on the hook for incentivizing your students and can instead focus on what's truly making it hard for them to meet expectations.

Question: So, what am I on the hook for?
Answer: Meeting your students where they're at and knowing what to do if they're struggling.

Question: So, all those stickers we've been doling out to encourage kids to meet our expectations . . .
Answer: They can't possibility help you understand or address what's making it hard for a student to meet an expectation. That's asking a lot of a sticker.

Question: Isn't it true that if a student is just motivated enough, they are capable of anything?
Answer: No, that's not true at all. All the incentivizing in the world doesn't help any of us meet expectations that are currently beyond our reach and doesn't help us exhibit a more adaptive frustration response. Invoking poor motivation when a kid is having difficulty meeting an expectation makes it harder for us to find out what's getting in the kid's way and harder to identify interventions that would actually work.

Question: Aren't stickers good for the kids who *are* meeting our expectations?
Answer: Not when you adopt one of the most important themes of this book: *Kids do well if they can*. Meaning if a kid *could* do well, they *would* do well. Because doing well is *preferable*. The kids who are getting

the stickers aren't meeting expectations because of the stickers. They're meeting expectations because they *can*. Why would we want to shift them from intrinsic motivation to extrinsic motivation?

Question: And all those detentions and suspensions and expulsions we've been doling out to discourage concerning behavior?
Answer: Now that you know that concerning behavior is a frustration response . . . and that frustration responses occur when a student is having difficulty meeting certain expectations . . . then you also know why detentions, suspensions, expulsions, corporal punishment, restraints, and seclusions are completely missing the mark and can be very counterproductive and harmful.

Question: I get the feeling you're not real keen on characterizations such as attention-seeking, manipulative, coercive, and unmotivated either.
Answer: Correct. All those characterizations are based on the belief that, somehow, doing poorly is working out better for a student than doing well would. Nonsense. Doing well is always preferable. Now you know concerning behavior communicates that a student is having difficulty meeting an expectation. It's not communicating poor motivation, except in the case of kids who have unremitting unsolved problems, have been on the receiving end of punitive, exclusionary discipline for a very long time, and have lost hope. Incentives aren't going to give those kids what they need either. We should stop using those terms. We should stop including them in our functional behavioral assessments (FBAs). We should also stop saying things like *"He could do it if he wanted to," "She needs to try harder,"* and *"They need to push through it."* Those statements let adults off the hook for the work we (and the student) need to do to find out what's making it hard for students to meet expectations and identify effective solutions together.

We'd Be Early, Not Late

As you'll read about in more detail in the next chapter, a lot of the training educators receive on how to handle students who are struggling teaches them what to do when those students are already, or at the precipice of, escalating. Since (as you'll soon see) the expectations students are having difficulty meeting are highly predictable, waiting for frustration responses before intervening is late, and very poor timing. In a classroom full of developmental variability where we're trying to meet every student where they're at, being late is not your best strategy. You'll want to have assessment practices, paperwork, structures, policies, and practices that point you toward being early. Sure, it's fine to know what to do when you didn't recognize that a student was having difficulty meeting an expectation until it was too late, but it's much better to know what to do so you aren't late in the first place.

We'd Be Collaborative, Not Unilateral

Educators are trained to be familiar with the myriad factors that could be interfering with a student completing a particular task or assignment, to decide which factors are coming into play for a particular student on a particular task, and then to apply interventions—such as supports, strategies, pre-teaching, finding the right entry point, adapting or adjusting the assignment—that will help the student overcome those assumed factors and ultimately complete the task or assignment. Educators typically come to these conclusions and apply these interventions *independent* of input from the intended beneficiaries (the students who are struggling to meet the expectations). We employ these interventions with great faith because they work. Sometimes. The bad news is that these practices *don't* work more often than we tend to acknowledge. What happens when they don't work? We move on to *other* hypotheses about what could be making it difficult for the student to meet the expectation and apply *additional* strategies and supports. This scenario could last an entire school year—or many—and, despite our best intentions and efforts, we might never hit the nail on the head.

When we don't hit the nail on the head over an extended period—as is the case with students who continue to struggle with certain expectations over weeks, months, or years—we are perpetually placing expectations on students that they are unable to meet and frequently wind up with students who are having difficulty meeting a rather large number of expectations. These students consequently become increasingly frustrated, often resulting in increasingly frequent and unlucky frustration responses. Their teachers become increasingly frustrated too.

It's hard to meet kids where they're at if you don't know where they're at. And the best source of information for identifying what's making it hard for a student to meet a given expectation is the student.

Question: Wait, what? Ask the student what's making it hard for them to meet an expectation?
Answer: That's right.

Question: What makes you think they know?
Answer: Thirty years of asking.

Question: What if they won't talk to you?
Answer: We find that if we stop talking with kids about their concerning behavior (*"Why did you tip over the desk in class?"*)—which is what we've always been talking to them about—and start talking with them about expectations they're having difficulty meeting (that are causing the concerning behavior), they do talk. Talking with kids about their concerning behavior just causes them to think they're in trouble, become defensive, and stop talking.

Question: What if they're nonspeaking?
Answer: They can participate—in one way or another—in helping us understand what's making it hard to meet an expectation and in helping us come up with solutions.

Question: You're going to tell us how to do that, yes?
Answer: Of course. Glad you're interested!

....

Let's use our imaginations for a moment. Let's imagine a scenario in which we are consumed by the developmental variability of our school and classroom, consumed with expectation management, obsessed with meeting every student where they're at, and less focused on a bar students must clear by the end of the school year. Let's image that each student is their own reference point for achievement and progress, that we aren't spending a lot of time thinking about things that are beyond our control, aren't mischaracterizing concerning behavior, aren't relying on poor motivation as our go-to explanation for a student's struggles and therefore aren't relying on motivational strategies to incentivize the student to perform. And let's imagine that we're rooting out everything we're doing that's late, consumed with thinking about how to be early instead, and are truly devoting ourselves to retooling the structures that push us toward being late.

You might be thinking, y'all have *quite* the imaginations! Perhaps, but there's no choice but to imagine how things could be different, especially for the students who are struggling. And, as you may have read in the Introduction, there are many schools that have moved from imagination to vision to action. Hopefully yours will do the same.

....

We've covered a lot of territory in this chapter. Here's a recap:

- *Developmental variability* is what's walking in the door, guaranteed. It applies to everything.
- *Meeting kids where they're at* is the definition of good teaching.
- Concerning behavior is a *frustration response* and communicates that a student is having difficulty meeting an expectation.
- We should be far more focused on the expectations kids are having difficulty meeting than the frustration responses that tell us they're having difficulty meeting them.
- Placing expectations on kids that we already know they can't meet is a good way to cause lots of frustration responses.
- Kids with unlucky frustration responses are struggling with certain skills; they are not poorly motivated.
- A lot of what educators are trained to do is late and unilateral. We need to create structures and practices that help educators be early and collaborative instead. And that journey begins in the next chapter.

Q & A

Question: Can you give me a quick definition of *developmental variability*?

Answer: Every student has different life experiences, different skills, and different learning styles, learns at different speeds, learns some things more easily than others, and approaches the school day with a different frame of mind. One size definitely does not fit all.

Question: And *expectation management*?

Answer: Make sure your expectations for each student are those that are in range for them. Don't place expectations on kids you're pretty certain they can't meet.

Question: That's not selling kids short?
Answer: No, that's meeting them where they're at.

Question: And it's OK to come back to an expectation once we think a kid can meet it?
Answer: Of course.

Question: Love what you're saying about developmental variability and meeting kids where they're at. And I love what you're saying about educators being among the most important socialization agents in our society. Are my special education director and principal going to support all that?
Answer: Many special education directors and principals are already OK with it. Hopefully the rest are reading this book. The conversations about how to help students who are struggling are already occurring. What's been lacking is a road map for change.

Question: The discussion of frustration responses was very helpful. And yet, I am still reminded of the academic grade-level expectations and outcomes we have in our buildings. Our parent-teacher conferences, team validation meetings, and IEP meetings are often focused on data looking at student academic growth, midyear benchmarks, and end-of-year benchmarks.
Answer: You can still talk about those things, so long as academic growth and benchmarks are individualized and discussed within the context of meeting kids where they're at.

Question: Should schools be spending less time looking at behavioral data and more time looking at academic and social expectations?
Answer: That would be a *very* positive step.

Question: So, relying less on motivational strategies . . . does that mean consequences are no longer in play?
Answer: As you've read, consequences aren't focused on solving the problems that are causing a student's concerning behavior; they're focused on modifying the behavior. And teaching and reteaching replacement behaviors and checking-in and checking-out (CICO) are focused on behavior as well.

Question: How about making amends?
Answer: While philosophically appealing, making amends—doing something restorative or to repair harm—doesn't solve any of the problems that are causing the behaviors that kids are making amends for.

Question: We talk with kids all the time in our school. So, I don't quite understand when you say that we're making a lot of decisions without the kids' input.
Answer: The talking you'll be learning about in forthcoming chapters is different from the talking adults usually do with kids. Often, we're talking *at* kids, often about their concerning behaviors, and telling them what they should have done instead. This is not that.

Question: I hope you're not saying that educators should be therapists.
Answer: No, we're not saying that educators should be therapists. But educators have always solved problems with their students. If you're still OK being a problem-solver, we should be good to go.

Question: And I hope you're not blaming educators.
Answer: It's not our style to blame anyone. Educators inherited a lot of the structures, systems, and practices that aren't working very well in schools. Questioning the things that aren't working and then changing them is better not only for students but for educators as well.

Closer Look: Concerning Behavior Is Informative

As you've now read, concerning behavior—whether it's whining, pouting, sulking, crying, screaming, swearing, hitting, spitting, kicking, biting, destroying, or just plain noncompliance—is the way in which kids (and other human beings) communicate that they're having difficulty meeting a particular expectation. So, at least in one very important respect—and we realize this is going to sound a little strange—concerning behavior is *good*: it alerts you to the fact that there's an expectation a student is having difficulty meeting; that they're struggling; that they're in distress. You want to know that, right?

And yet, as you read above, many adults respond to concerning behavior by trying to *extinguish* it—through punishment and/or by ignoring the child—and by *insisting harder* that a student meet an expectation they're having difficulty meeting. The latter is a fascinating approach, because there's really no reason to think that insisting harder is going to help a student overcome whatever hurdle was making it hard for them to meet the expectation in the first place. And why would we want to punish or ignore the behaviors that signal that a child is frustrated or in distress?

Some adults are *offended* by students' concerning behavior—they take it personally—often because they're interpreting the behavior as willful, intentional, purposeful, and goal-oriented (the student is *choosing* not to meet the expectation). That can cause them to respond in ways that are quite counterproductive. Still other adults view noncompliance as a threat to their authority and set about the task of using power—typically in the form of consequences—to convince the student that they must comply, often fueled by the belief that concerning behavior must be dealt with decisively and immediately, so as to make the clearest possible connection between the behavior and its consequences. But consequences don't solve any problems; they just modify the behaviors that are being caused by those problems. We've done a lot of harm to a lot of kids by interpreting their concerning behavior inaccurately.

So, while those unlucky concerning behaviors can be unsafe and disruptive, and while you don't want to let them continue, there's more than one way to improve behavior, and some are way more effective than others. In this book, you'll be learning how to improve behavior by *solving the problems that are causing it.*

Instead of relying on consequences to reduce concerning behavior, you're instead *proactively* identifying the expectations a student is having difficulty reliably meeting (you'll learn how in chapter 4), *proactively* gathering information from the student to figure out what's making it hard for them to meet the expectation (doing that proactively is much better than in the heat of the moment, and involving the student in that process is much better than doing it all by yourself), and *proactively* collaborating with the student on a solution (we find that those solutions tend to work better than the ones we adults come up with on our own). And it sure would be nice if we had structures in place to facilitate those things.

All in due course. This is only chapter 2. Fortunately, there's the rest of the book.

....

"To empathize is not to condone, and to explain is not to excuse."

—Jonathan Lie

3

Set Up to Be Late

Jackson came in from recess still agitated over a disagreement he'd had with a classmate on the playground. It didn't help that math, his worst subject, always followed recess. Though he was officially in the fourth grade, he was still testing at a first-grade level in math. The teachers in his special education classroom were under pressure to have him do some form of grade-level math work—they didn't want to be perceived as depriving him of educational opportunities—but despite countless accommodations, strategies, and adaptations to his assignments, math was still a major source of frustration and always had the potential to set him off.

His paraprofessional put a worksheet in front of Jackson and told him she'd be back to help him with it.

Jackson took a quick glance at the worksheet and promptly announced, to no one in particular, "I'm not doing it."

"Jackson, hold tight, I'll be right back," said the para.

Jackson slouched at his desk until the para returned. "Something happen during recess?" she asked, sitting down next to him.

"Dante is a dick," said Jackson. Fortunately, Dante was working out of earshot at a computer.

"Jackson, don't forget about how we're trying to be kind to each other," said the para. "Shall we try to get some math done?"

"I'm not doing it," said Jackson. "And you should talk to Dante about being kind."

"Well, math is what we're doing right now," said the para. "All your classmates are doing their math."

"Good for them," Jackson mumbled.

The para arranged the worksheet in front of Jackson. "Come on, let's do a few. I'll help you."

Jackson pushed his chair back from the desk. "No."

"What color are you right now?" asked the para, referring to a rating system aimed at helping kids self-assess their level of regulation.

"Black," mumbled Jackson, naming a shade that isn't one of the colors in the rating system.

"Jackson, do you need to use your strategies to get unstuck?"

"I need you to leave me alone," said Jackson.

"Maybe we should go to the Calming Corner," suggested the paraprofessional.

Jackson rose from his seat. He began walking slowly to the door of the classroom—the opposite direction of the Calming Corner—now drawing the attention of the classroom teacher, who was helping another student.

"Jackson, please go back and sit down at your seat," said the teacher, as she quickly positioned herself between Jackson and the door.

Gathering steam, Jackson tried to physically force his way through the teacher to the door. At ninety-five pounds, he elicited a slight grunt from the teacher but made scant progress. Because Jackson had run out of the school several times into a busy street, the teacher and para felt his attempt to escape the classroom was an issue of imminent harm. With knowing glances, they commenced wrestling Jackson to the ground, quickly joined by the ed tech.

"No!" yelled Jackson.

The takedown, or restraint, would have been a fairly efficient process had Jackson gone down willingly. But graciously accepting being pinned to the ground wasn't his M.O. He tried to head-butt the teacher and managed to scratch the arm of the para. The teacher used her walkie-talkie to alert the office to the situation.

"Let me up!" yelled Jackson, breathing heavily, still trying to escape the grasp of the three adults.

"We don't like this any more than you do," said the para.

"Let me up!" Jackson said, teeth gritted, half crying, half seething.

"We'll let you up when you calm down and agree to do your math," said the teacher.

The principal arrived on the scene, immediately noting that the three adults had Jackson reasonably well-contained on the ground. "Anyone need any help?"

"If you could get everyone back to work, that would be great," said the teacher.

The other seven kids in the classroom were, it appeared, unfazed by the transpiring events. It was not unusual for Jackson to be restrained (his teachers tended to choose restraining over secluding, as Jackson took even longer to calm down in a seclusion room). This was his fifteenth restraint of the year, and it was only November. Some of his classmates had been restrained or secluded as well. Though the staff in the special education classroom had received training on trauma-informed care during the summer, their restraint numbers were even higher than the same time a year ago.

"Get off me!" yelled Jackson.

"You need to calm down first," said the teacher.

Eventually, after about fifteen minutes, Jackson calmed enough for the three adults to allow him to get off the floor. He returned to his seat and immediately crumpled up the math worksheet.

....

Caregivers have highly variable reactions to the above scenario:

"Kid got what he had coming to him."

"Can't let one kid ruin it for the rest."

"Gotta hold kids accountable."

"You can't just let him off the hook from doing the math."

"De-escalating, restraining, and secluding are just part of everyday life in a special education classroom. It's the way we've always done it."

"What do you expect us to do with these kids who are completely out of control?"

"Couldn't the adults have de-escalated the situation more effectively?"

"Was the restraint executed properly?"

"No one wants to restrain a kid. That must have been very unpleasant for the adults."

"No kid wants to be restrained or secluded. That must have been very scary and unpleasant for Jackson."

"Can he actually do *the math they're insisting that he do?"*

"It's fortunate that Jackson didn't die."

We understand the sentiment behind all the reactions, though the final four resonate the most with your authors. That last one might seem extreme, except for the fact that a study published in 2021 documented seventy-nine deaths of kids while being restrained over a twenty-six-year period in the United States, lending an even more tragic connotation to the word "late."* They were suffocated.

---

* M. A. Nunno, et al. "A 26-Year Study of Restraint Fatalities Among Children and Adolescents in the United States: A Failure of Organizational Structures and Processes," *Child & Youth Care Forum* 51 (2022): 661–80. https://doi.org/10.1007/s10566-021-09646-w.

De-escalating, restraining, and secluding will not help us be responsive to the developmental variability inherent in our classrooms. And yet, for decades, we've been training educators to de-escalate and restrain kids (there is no formal training for using seclusion rooms), ostensibly for purposes of "preventing" crises and keeping kids, their classmates, and their caregivers safe. Such training is standard fare in many school systems.

From the outside looking in, such procedures may seem necessary. After all, it *is* important to keep the "out of control" kids from harming others and detracting from the learning of their classmates. Even on the inside, many educators—and some of their national teacher unions—still believe that de-escalating, restraining, and secluding kids are simply accepted practices for special education classrooms and students.

But others know that there are a ton of problems with this picture. First, there are a lot of schools and treatment facilities serving kids with equally concerning behaviors that don't use restraint or seclusion. So apparently those practices *aren't* necessary and are *not* the way everyone has always done it. Second, there are no data to suggest that de-escalating, restraining, and secluding kids keep anyone safer. Indeed, the study cited above suggests quite the opposite. Death is only the most extreme outcome of these practices and doesn't account for the untold physical and emotional injuries suffered by kids and staff when such practices are utilized. Third, such procedures are disproportionately applied to students with disabilities and those with black and brown skin, meaning that this is also a social justice issue. Fourth, de-escalation, restraint, and seclusion can hardly be characterized as crisis *prevention* strategies; as you've read, they occur very late in a sequence of events that begins with an *expectation a student is having difficulty meeting* (as depicted in the graphic below).

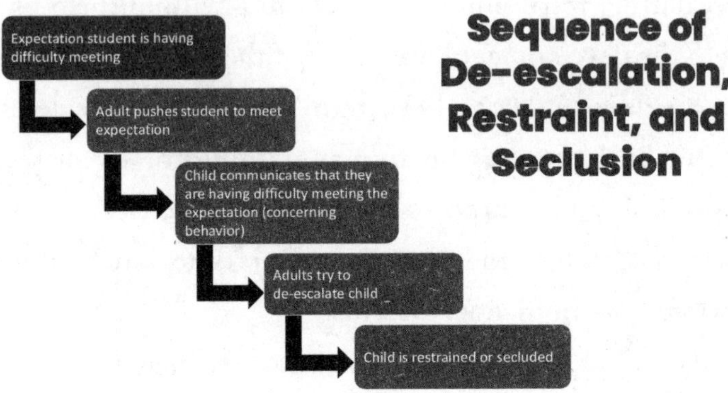

In the first bubble, the student is having difficulty meeting an expectation. That's seldom surprising, since the expectation has probably gone unmet for a very long time (an unmet expectation is only a surprise the first time; it's not a surprise after that). As you know, due to a variety of factors—human nature included—adults often respond to such unmet expectations by pushing students harder to meet the expectation they already know the student can't reliably meet (the second bubble). Pushing kids harder to meet expectations they can't reliably meet *increases* the likelihood that a student will exhibit a *frustration response* (concerning behavior; that's the third bubble). It's important to reiterate that the frustration response is *late* (the student is already having difficulty meeting the expectation, and, again, it's not the first time). At that point in the sequence caregivers might resort to strategies they learned in the de-escalation training they receive every year (bubble number four). When de-escalating doesn't accomplish the mission, restraint or seclusion (bubble number five) often follows and seems justifiable and necessary. But the fact that de-escalating, restraining, and secluding occur very late in a highly predictable sequence indicates that they aren't crisis prevention strategies at all; they're crisis *management* strategies.

What's not depicted in the graphic is what comes next, interventions that are later still, including punitive, exclusionary disciplinary practices such as detention, suspension, corporal punishment, and, if the adults have finally had it with the student, expulsion or placement in a special purpose school (where de-escalating, restraining, and secluding kids are often even more likely to occur).

Who's on the receiving end of these interventions the most? The kids who aren't doing OK. To save these students from ongoing harm and inexorable decline, and educators from interminable frustration and desperation, we need to stop being late. That means we need to start focusing on the first bubble: the expectations we're placing on students and what we do if they're having difficulty meeting them. As you've read, those unmet expectations—we'll be calling them *unsolved problems*—can be identified proactively (we'll describe how that's done in the next chapter) and can therefore be solved proactively (we'll describe how that's done after that) or temporarily put on hold (since it won't be possible to solve all the problems at once). In other words, we'll be delineating a technology for being *early*, a much more legitimate definition of crisis *prevention*.

We should mention that the "restraint industrial complex," as it's been called, is highly profitable. The largest of the companies providing training to school systems on de-escalating and restraining kids—the Crisis Prevention Institute (CPI)—generates about $100 million every year, a number that undoubtedly appeals to its private equity owners. Shockingly (to the degree that we're shocked by anything anymore), there are organizations claiming to advocate *against* restraint and seclusion that take money from and/or partner with CPI.

By the way, as Alfie Kohn and his colleagues underscored back in 2002 in their book *Education, Inc.: Turning Learning into a Business* (2002), there are many other realms in which capitalism has been the cart leading the horse of American education, with high-stakes testing very much in the mix as well.

Whole Lotta Late

It's not just de-escalating, restraining, secluding, and punitive, exclusionary discipline that are late. In the belief that it's important to appreciate the scope of the situation before we start to remedy it, let's take a brief tour of all the other things that go on in schools that are late. Their popularity notwithstanding, the late interventions described below do not represent best practices. They're just the things we do because we aren't set up to be early. But being late is not a given. We don't have to keep running around like chickens with their heads cut off, bouncing from one crisis to another.

De-escalating: You've read about this one already. But we're putting it at the top of our list because some people think (and companies are telling them) that de-escalating is as early as it gets. Now you know better. Again, by the time a student is being de-escalated you're quite late. So, while it's fine to train educators on how to de-escalate, it's way better to train them on how to keep students from becoming escalated in the first place.

Breaks: We're giving students a lot of breaks these days. We're not referring here to *planned* breaks (e.g., work for ten minutes, take a break for two), but rather the breaks we give students when they begin to struggle, usually with an academic task. (By the way, the word "when" is usually a dead ringer for being late, as in *"What should we do when . . . ?"*) Since the student is *already* struggling with the task—and has almost certainly struggled with the task previously—taking a break is late. Not only is the break late, it's also *not going to solve the problem that necessitated the break.* That explains why some students are getting fifteen to twenty breaks a day. Those breaks take a lot of time. What would it look like if we swapped out all the time we're spending on breaks and spent a fraction of that time solving the problems that are precipitating the breaks?

Calming Corners/Sensory Rooms: When do kids access the Calming Corner? When they're not calm. When are they not calm? When they're already having difficulty meeting an expectation. Accessing the Calming Corner is not only late but also won't solve the problem that necessitated the trip to the Calming Corner in the first place. Admirably, some schools have been replacing Calming Corners with sensory rooms, which is conceptually a step in a more humane direction but—especially if they're being used in the same way as Calming Corners—still late. Escorting kids to and monitoring them in the Calming Corner or sensory room takes a lot of time. What mentalities and structures would we need to change so that staff could proactively identify and solve problems with students so they didn't need to access the Calming Corner or sensory room in the first place? How much time would that save?

Calling for the Late Staff: Many schools have staff members whose official job it is to show up on the scene when a student has escalated in response to an unsolved problem. Titles vary widely (crisis management specialist, behavior management specialist, etc.), but you know who you are. And, of course, there are other staff—principal, assistant principal, school psychologist, school counselor, school social worker, ed tech, paraprofessional, Board Certified Behavior Analyst (BCBA)—whose job titles don't necessarily infer lateness but who are nonetheless relied upon to show up when it's already late. What would it look like if we did a complete one-eighty and figured out how to help everyone in the school proactively identify and solve problems with students? Then we'd all be the Early Staff.

Walkie-Talkies: These have become ubiquitous in schools, especially in the U.S., and they can be useful to communicate about school goings-on, such as bus arrivals and departures or serious emergencies. But they are also relied upon to call for help when students have become escalated. Just like in *It's a Wonderful Life*, where the ringing bell signifies that an angel is getting its wings, the walkie-talkie squawking in a school usually signifies that we're late, which is not so wonderful.

Room Clears: Clearing the room to ensure safety when a highly predictable unsolved problem has caused a student to spin out of control (yet again) is late. Room clears take a lot of time away from learning, and they don't solve the problems that cause kids to spin out of control. Which means that, in the absence of solving those problems, the next room clear is only minutes or hours away.

Reset: This can refer to a process (giving a kid time to collect themselves after a concerning behavior) or a specific location, sometimes as an alternative to expulsion or suspension. Whether a process or a location, resets come into play *after* a kid has already become escalated. By the time we're resetting, we're late. Could the time we're spending on resetting be devoted to solving problems proactively? Why aren't we doing that instead?

Debriefing: Sometimes used as part of the resetting process, the goal is to have a student reflect on what caused them to become upset, collect themselves, think about what they could have done differently (when it was already late), and get back to class as quickly as possible. But reflecting on and considering replacement behaviors are insufficient, since they don't solve the problem that caused the student to get upset in the first place. Which means they're just going to escalate again the next time the problem arises, which means we're going to be debriefing again. And again.

Call the Parents: Home–school communication is a wonderful thing. It's very important that parents have a sense of what's going on at school, and especially of the unsolved problems school staff are trying to solve with a student. But communication with parents of students with concerning behaviors is often strongly slanted toward the concerning *behaviors* their child is exhibiting. Many parents anxiously dread the phone ringing during the school day, certain that it's yet another demand for their child to be retrieved because of yet another episode. The parents typically have no clue about the unsolved problem that caused the behaviors and—this is important—*are not well-positioned to solve that problem even if they did know,* since it's not their expectation. But many parents—eager to disprove the view that they are passive, permissive, inconsistent, noncontingent, neglectful disciplinarians (the traditional and still quite popular view of parents of kids with concerning behavior)—respond by lowering the boom on the kid when concerning behavior is reported at school. Now we have a double-whammy: the kid is being punished both at school *and* home, and *no amount* of punishment is going to solve the problems that are causing the behaviors the kid is being punished for. For purposes of our current discussion, calling the parent about a student's concerning behavior is both late and focused on what's late. Parents are on the hook for the expectations their child is having difficulty meeting at home. The school folks are on the hook for the expectations the child is having difficulty meeting at school.

Emphasis on Restorative Practices: Aren't restorative practices intended to replace punitive, exclusionary discipline and improve school culture? Well, yes . . . and restorative practices are great at creating a healthy school culture and climate. But, as you've read, by the time a student is making amends or doing something restorative, we're late. And, as you've also read, making amends doesn't solve any of the problems that are causing the behaviors for which a student is making amends.

Teaching Coping Strategies: If you're teaching a student to cope with frustration—by taking deep breaths, counting to ten, and self-assessing their level of regulation—you're teaching them what to do when it's already late. While coping with frustration is a useful skill, teaching kids how to do it should comprise only a small percentage of the coping strategies we're helping kids develop. The lion's share should be helping them learn how to anticipate and solve problems so they don't get frustrated in the first place.

But isn't frustration necessary for fostering grit? We have our doubts. Grit is defined by psychologist Angela Duckworth as *passion and perseverance for long-term goals.* And it's great that a lot of educators feel it's their job to help kids develop passion for their goals and persevere through frustration. But all the passion and perseverance in the world isn't going help kids solve the problems that are causing their frustration in the first place. We're biased, of course, but we think there are *three* Ps involved in developing grit: problem-solving, passion, and perseverance. And we think the first P is far and away the most important.

Emphasis on Co-Regulating: A lot of the co-regulating literature is focused on having adults prepare in advance to stay calm when a kid is becoming or has already escalated. The prep might be early, but it kicks in when it's late.

Functional Behavior Assessments (FBAs): Because FBAs are focused on behavior, they're focused on what's late and therefore set the stage for being late. They don't have to be focused on behavior, but most are.

Discipline Referrals, Detentions, Suspensions, Expulsions: We're being repetitive, but we wanted to provide a comprehensive list in this section. These are all late and are all responses to concerning behavior. None solves the problems that are causing a student's concerning behavior.

Restraining and Secluding: Again, redundant, but we don't want to leave any lateness left unmentioned. Though this seems like a good time to ask why any kid would want to go to a school where they're being restrained and secluded. And why any educator would want to work in a school where the "option of last resort" is so common.

School Resource Officers (SROs): In communities, the police generally show up when it's already late. Things are really no different in schools.

How Did We Get Here?

Why do we find ourselves downstream, managing crises so often? How did we become so fixated on what to do when it's already late? Lots of places to look for the answer to that question.

Training: It's not just that a lot of the training we've been providing educators has been focused on what to do once it's already late, it's that being late is also at the foundation of traditional classroom management and school disciplinary practices. For decades, we've been inundating schools with Board Certified Behavior Analysts, yet another industry, one that generates around $4 billion annually in the U.S., who are primarily trained to focus on kids' concerning behaviors and modify those behaviors. As we established above, if we're focused on a student's concerning behavior, we're focused on what's late. (It's important to mention that many BCBAs support what you're reading in this book, but it's also the case that many do not.)

A related industry, Positive Behavioral Interventions and Supports (PBIS), heavily supported by the U.S. Department of Education (which isn't supposed to endorse anything), is ubiquitous in schools and also derives from the behavior analytic tradition. Thanks to PBIS (called PBL, PBS, or PB4L in countries outside the U.S.), assessment practices in schools, especially when it comes to students who are struggling behaviorally, have been centered on their concerning behavior: *behavior* checklists, *behavior* observations, functional *behavior* assessments (FBAs), *behavior* intervention plans (BIPs). And intervention practices—teaching, reteaching, and rewarding replacement *behaviors*, checking-in and checking-out (about the *behaviors*), punishing maladaptive *behaviors* (students being deprived of recess, being held after school, detention, in-school or out-of-school suspension, expulsion, corporal punishment)—are also focused on what's late. It's the Late Show.

Capitalism: As you read above, there's big money in training educators to de-escalate and restrain kids, modify behavior, and teach late coping skills, and there are many companies eager to sell such programs to schools. Regrettably, all too many schools and school systems have been willing and unquestioning customers.

The Kids Who *Are* Doing OK: It's seductive to believe that most of what's going on in a school is working if most of the students are doing well. And despite various policies and initiatives that have made it harder for educators to do their jobs, there are lots of good things going on in schools and lots of things are going well. But, as the saying goes, looks can be deceiving. The kids who are doing well do suffer when, because of the concerning behaviors of one of their classmates, they feel unsafe or their learning is disrupted. And it's not good for them to see their classmates with concerning behavior treated in ways that are harmful and counterproductive. So just because a lot of kids are doing OK doesn't mean we're home free.

Unlucky Frustration Responses: Classrooms are busy places. Classroom teachers are busy people. Because they can be scary, disruptive, and dangerous, unlucky frustration responses are sure to grab a teacher's attention. (By the way, this is the one way in which lucky frustration responses are unlucky: they're less likely to be noticed. Of course, if we're focused on unsolved problems rather than frustration responses, the lucky and unlucky part becomes far less important.) Some things can wait, but not unlucky frustration responses. So, there's bound to be quite the demand for handling those frustration responses. Now you know that demand is misplaced; the demand should instead be on practices that occur far earlier.

....

Suffice to say that many kids and educators have been suffering unnecessarily because of policies, structures, and practices that push us toward being late. We need to question those policies, structures, and practices. They're like a familiar, old, frayed sweater that we keep wearing even though it doesn't fit anymore. And because there's been no well-disseminated technology for being *early*—moving *upstream*—we need to make sure that educators know what to do instead.

In the coming chapters, we'll be describing how to *truly* prevent crises: by proactively identifying the expectations students are having difficulty meeting (again, called *unsolved problems*); giving serious consideration to whether students are actually able to meet the expectations that are being placed upon them (again, what we call *expectation management*); and proactively prioritizing those problems (so we're not working on everything at once) and proactively solving those problems (or putting some on hold for now) so kids don't become escalated in the first place. In doing these things, behavior and safety are improved, academics do not suffer, test scores do not decrease, time is saved, relationships and communication are enhanced, and culture and climate are improved. And best of all, educators and kids stop getting harmed.

Q & A

Question: I'm a bit blown away by all the things we do in schools that are late. That's demoralizing. But I love the idea of being early. It seems like moving upstream should be a very high priority.
Answer: We agree. But given all the structures and practices that are pointing you toward being late, it's going to take some doing. It would be great if your teachers' unions were on board as well.

Question: I get that we're late a lot. But, in my building, we often have strategies in place before behaviors escalate. And yet it often feels like we are still playing catch-up. And we have lots of meetings with parents so we can be prepared for a student's difficulties before they start escalating. Sometimes there are changes in a student's home impacting them at school that can be difficult for us to tease out. This requires a lot of proactive communication between schools and home. How can we be earlier with parents and families without imposing ourselves into their personal lives?
Answer: No doubt, there are schools that are trying hard to be proactive. But if they're still focused on a student's concerning *behavior*—rather than on the problems that are causing that behavior—they're still going to be late. And if the solutions they are applying are unilateral, then a very important voice—the student's—is still missing. Parents are often quite receptive to home–school communication, especially if they don't feel blamed or judged for their child's concerning behavior. It's critical for parents to know that the folks at school need to be apprised of changes in medication or any life events that could be impacting their child at school. And for many of our most vulnerable students, communication between home and school needs to be *daily*, in both directions.

Question: So, I get that we shouldn't be using restraint and seclusion, though I'm still skeptical about eliminating it completely, given the difficult profiles of many of our students.
Answer: We'd be surprised if you weren't skeptical, especially given your current reality. But we can change your reality. If you read this book all the way through and implement what you're reading, the proof will be in the pudding.

Question: And we're also getting rid of detentions, suspensions, expulsions, and corporal punishment?
Answer: As you've read, punitive disciplinary practices don't solve any of the problems that are causing kids' concerning behaviors. That's why it's the same ten to fifteen kids in every school who are on the receiving end of most of the punitive, exclusionary disciplinary practices doled out in that building. In other words, the kids who access the school discipline program the most are the ones who benefit from it the least. And the ones who aren't accessing the school discipline program don't need it in the first place. That's a system that's working for no one. And it is appalling that we're still hitting kids at school with a twenty-four-inch piece of plywood in seventeen states in the U.S.

Question: Wait, you don't think the well-behaved kids are behaving themselves because of the school discipline program?
Answer: No, we don't. Kids do well if they can, not because of the school discipline program.

Closer Look: Where Does the National Education Association Stand on Restraint and Seclusion?

In its Crisis Mitigation guidelines, the National Education Association (NEA)—the largest labor union in the United States—provides guidance on handling crises in schools. The guide clumps together a wide array of crises schools may face, including natural disasters, fires, gas leaks, active shooters, bomb threats, the death of a student or faculty member, and . . . concerning behavior. As regards the latter, the guidelines rely heavily on the traditional definition of the function of a child's behavior (e.g., attention seeking, escaping, avoiding, tangible rewards).

By the way, it's not that the traditional definition of function is wrong, it just doesn't go far enough. We *all* get, escape, and avoid, so concluding that a student is doing so doesn't distinguish the student from the rest of us. You've already read about the true function of a student's concerning behavior: *it communicates that there are expectations the student is having difficulty meeting.* Those are the problems that need to be solved. That being the case, "get, escape, and avoid" shouldn't be the end of the conversation; if we're focused on unsolved problems, it doesn't even need to be the beginning.

But we digress. The guidance on crisis management in the NEA's Crisis Mitigation Guidelines is straight from the playbook of the Crisis Prevention Institute; indeed, those seeking more information are referred to the CPI website:

> *There are various de-escalation responses that can be used with students depending on their age, ability to understand, and state of anger or potential threat.*
>
> - *Without talking, present yourself in a non-threatening posture, preferably at an angle to the student, not face-to-face. Keep your arms at your side, open palms, and begin deep breathing. The breathing will keep you calm and model a way for the student to reach calmness as well.*

- *Use short, factual statements such as "You're angry. What can I do to help?" in a respectful tone of voice.*
- *If the student verbalizes what's going on, use nonverbal gestures to indicate listening and understanding: nodding, appropriate facial expressions, and making eye contact, with attention to cultural sensitivities. Encourage giving words to feelings.*
- *Be mindful of your physical proximity to the student. Allow the student to determine how close is too close.*
- *As the tension eases, use statements that shift the student up and out of the anger to a place of readiness to move forward in a safe way. Ask the student for a suggestion as to what to do next or offer one that will provide security and avoid embarrassment.*
- *At a later time, process the event with the student, parents/guardians, school counselor, or other adults who can support the student. Document the incident.*
- *Be aware of and avoid responses that will escalate a threatening situation, such as raising your voice; displaying body language that conveys frustration, anger, or threats; creating a power struggle through the use of sarcasm, patronizing tone, or giving orders; bringing up past history or events, placing blame, making comparisons to others, and encroaching on personal space.*

These guidelines lead us to believe that the NEA hasn't thought enough about how to prevent concerning behavior in schools to better protect its members and their students. We think that's a shame. And we think the members and the kids deserve better.

The NEA has also remained steadfastly neutral on federal legislation—especially the Keeping All Students Safe Act (KASSA)—

aimed at reducing or eliminating the use of restraint and seclusion in schools. That may, at least partially, account for why such legislation has gained no traction since 2011. The fact that the NEA's guidance for educators references CPI directly should give all of us pause. We hope there's not more to that association than meets the eye.

The second-largest teachers' union in the US, the American Federation of Teachers, doesn't get a free pass either. It has remained neutral on federal legislation aimed at reducing the use of restraint and seclusion in American public schools.

....

"History is a vast early warning system."

—Norman Cousins

"An ounce of prevention is worth a pound of cure."

—Benjamin Franklin

4

Moving Upstream

In this chapter, we take our first steps toward being early. We're hoping you're energized by the realization that being late consumes massive amounts of time, compromises safety, and detracts from learning . . . and that things could be different. What do we need to change?

There's one major thing we need to adjust. Many subsequent adjustments flow from this first one. *We need to start focusing on unsolved problems (and solving them) and stop focusing on concerning behaviors (and modifying them).* And we need to identify those unsolved problems proactively so we can solve them proactively. Otherwise, we'll always find ourselves in the heat of the moment dealing with the frustration responses that are being caused by those unsolved problems. *This is a huge shift.*

As you've read, a lot of the assessment instrumentation used in schools for students who are struggling is focused on their concerning *behavior.* As you've also read, those assessment practices cause us to focus on what's late, greatly increasing the likelihood that our interventions will be late as well. Not coincidentally, we spend a lot of time *talking* about behavior too:

"Wait till you hear what Elena did today during recess when the kids wouldn't let her join in on the foursquare game!"

"Tommy put his fist through the window this afternoon during essay-writing in ELA."

"Jackson tried to bolt the classroom during math today. Took about fifteen minutes of restraining him to calm him down. And then he still wouldn't do his math!"

We also spend a lot of time talking about psychiatric diagnoses, which are just long lists of concerning behaviors. Diagnoses may be *descriptive* but they're not *explanatory*. Vast knowledge of psychiatric diagnoses is not a prerequisite for helping kids who aren't OK. Regrettably, psychiatric diagnoses are sometimes necessary for ensuring that a student gets the services we already know they need. That, of course, works to the disadvantage of the kids who are struggling and badly need our help but don't meet diagnostic criteria for any psychiatric disorder.

We also spend a lot of time *theorizing* about what's making it hard for a student to meet certain expectations and hard for them to respond to that frustration adaptively:

"Angela has been really difficult since her parents' divorce. Although now that I think of it, she wasn't an angel before they got divorced, either."

"You know, it doesn't surprise me that Kevin comes in hot in the morning. I can only imagine what mornings are like in that family."

"This school is in a very tough neighborhood. Need I say more?"

The problem with theories, aside from the fact that we're wrong a lot, and that we spend a lot of time talking about them, is that they often aren't *actionable*. We don't want to spend our meetings talking about the things about which we can do *nothing*. We want to spend our meetings talking about the things about which we can do *something*.

Finally, we spend a great deal of time talking about the supports and services students might need. Those are, of course, very important conversations, but as you'll read in much greater detail in chapter 6, timing is everything. This may sound like a statement of the obvious, but we really shouldn't be talking about supports and services until we know what a student needs. And yet, often, the support and services cart ends up in front of the horse.

If we're going to move beyond focusing on frustration responses and start talking about the problems that are causing them, we're going to need different assessment instrumentation. Toward that end, we're pleased to introduce you to the Assessment of Skills and Unsolved Problems (ASUP). It's going to give you the information that's been missing (skills and unsolved problems).

ASUP 2024

ASSESSMENT OF SKILLS AND UNSOLVED PROBLEMS

Collaborative & Proactive Solutions
THIS IS HOW PROBLEMS GET SOLVED

CHILD'S NAME: DATE:

NAMES OF CAREGIVERS COMPLETING THIS INSTRUMENT:

STEP 1: SKILLS

Whether neurotypical or neurodivergent, children communicate that they're having difficulty meeting expectations in diverse ways, including through their concerning behavior. This behavior is best conceived as a frustration or stress response, the nature of which is determined by a variety of factors, most especially certain skills related to flexibility/adaptability, frustration tolerance, problem solving, and emotion regulation. Some kids can demonstrate these skills under some conditions but not under other conditions.

This section is aimed at helping caregivers discuss those skills and the degree to which they may be impacting a particular child. Being aware of and considering the skills that may impact a child's capacity to handle life's problems and frustrations and meet various expectations helps caregivers move away from motivational explanations for concerning behavior (e.g. attention-seeking, manipulative, coercive, unmotivated) and toward a more compassionate, accurate understanding of such behavior. Note that these skills are not the primary focal point of intervention in the CPS model; the unsolved problems you'll be identifying in Step 2 will be the "targets" of intervention.

Please check off a skill if it's difficult for the child to access at times and appears to be making it difficult for the child to handle problems and frustrations and/or meet certain expectations:

- ○ Maintain focus
- ○ Regulate activity level
- ○ Handle transitions, shift from one mindset to another
- ○ Consider the likely outcomes or consequences of actions (impulse control)
- ○ Persist on challenging or tedious tasks
- ○ Sense of time (time that has passed, time needed)
- ○ Consider a range of solutions to problems
- ○ Flexibly handle ambiguity, uncertainty
- ○ Shift from original idea, plan, or solution
- ○ Express concerns, needs, or thoughts in words or other means of communication
- ○ Understand what is being communicated by others
- ○ Appreciate how their actions affect others
- ○ Regulate emotional response to problems and frustrations
- ○ Empathize with others, appreciate another person's perspective or point of view
- ○ Interoception (ability to understand and feel what's going on inside their body)
- ○ Tolerate and manage the sensory environment

STEP 2: UNSOLVED PROBLEMS

Unsolved problems are the specific expectations a child is having difficulty meeting. The wording of an unsolved problem will translate directly into the words that you'll be using when you introduce the unsolved problem to the child when it comes time to solve the problem together. Poorly worded unsolved problems often cause the problem-solving process to deteriorate before it even gets started. Please reference the ASUP Guide for guidance on writing unsolved problems.

SCHOOL/FACILITY PROMPTS

Are there specific tasks/expectations the student is having difficulty completing or getting started on?

Are there classmates this student is having difficulty getting along with in specific conditions?

Are there tasks and activities this student is having difficulty moving from or to?

Are there classes/activities the student is having difficulty attending/being on time to?

As you think about the start of the day to the end, are there any other expectations the student has difficulty reliably meeting or that you find yourself frequently reminding the child about?

HOME/CLINIC PROMPTS

Are there chores/tasks/activities the child is having difficulty completing or getting started on?

Are there siblings/other children the child is having difficulty getting along with in specific conditions?

Are there aspects of hygiene the child is having difficulty completing?

Are there activities the child is having difficulty ending or tasks the child is having difficulty moving on to?

As you think about the start of the day to the end, are there any other expectations the child has difficulty reliably meeting or that you find yourself frequently reminding the child about?

List unsolved problems here:
(or on a separate sheet)

LIVESINTHEBALANCE.ORG

LIVES IN THE BALANCE

The ASUP should be the standard pre-referral, triage instrument in every school system. The ASUP is going to write your Individualized Education Plan (IEP) for you. It's going to write your functional behavioral assessment (FBA) for you, so if you must do an FBA, complete the ASUP first. If you don't have to write an FBA, just complete the ASUP. The ASUP is going to save you a lot of time. You can find examples of ASUP-influenced FBAs, IEPs, and BIPs (behavior intervention plans) on the Lives in the Balance website (www.livesinthebalance.org). For the unfamiliar, Lives in the Balance is the hub of the Collaborative & Proactive Solutions (CPS) model that you're reading about in this book, and its website contains a ton of free resources and support.

Recall that kids (and adults) who are struggling with certain skills tend to have difficulty responding adaptively to problems and frustrations. The top section of the ASUP is going to help staff recognize that. You'll see in that section that there are sixteen skills listed, most derived from those global skills—flexibility/adaptability, frustration tolerance, problem-solving, and emotion regulation—we talked about in chapter 2. The bottom section is going to help staff identify every single expectation a student is having difficulty reliably meeting at school. Unsolved problems are early and actionable; once identified, they can be solved proactively. Identifying unsolved problems also helps staff come to recognize that a student's difficulties are highly predictable. And solved problems don't cause concerning behaviors, only unsolved problems do, so once those unsolved problems no longer set in motion a frustration response, there is no need for de-escalating, restraining, secluding, suspending, expelling, and hitting kids.

Do you need an ASUP on every kid in your building? Only if your student body is primarily comprised of the kids who aren't OK. In most general education settings, there are probably ten to fifteen kids who are struggling the most, getting in trouble the most, and accessing the school discipline program the most. The ones who account for 70 to 80 percent of discipline referrals and the punitive, exclusionary interventions that follow those referrals. The ones we're in the midst of losing. Those students need you to complete the ASUP, ASAP.

The ASUP was designed to be a discussion guide, not a freestanding checklist or rating scale. It's not criminal for a classroom teacher to complete the ASUP on their own, but it's far preferable that the ASUP be used in a formal meeting so that staff—hopefully, anyone in the building who works with the student—can start wearing shared lenses, speaking the same language, and getting on the same page. Otherwise, the left hand doesn't know what the right hand is doing, there is no continuity of care, and staff are relegated to an approach to intervention known as "winging it." The ASUP tends to be very persuasive for staff who still have traditional beliefs about the causes of concerning behavior. It is worth the logistical hurdles to find a way for everyone who works with a particular student to attend the ASUP meeting. ASUP meetings tend to require about forty-five minutes, especially if you're focused exclusively on identifying skills and unsolved problems. If you detour into theories, behaviors, stories, and so forth, ASUP meetings take forever.

There are no normative data for the ASUP, nor are there grade- or age- or gender-referenced percentiles. The student is their own reference point.

The student doesn't attend the ASUP meeting. There's no advantage to having the student sit through listening to adults talking about their unsolved problems and the skills with which they're struggling.

During an ASUP meeting, each participant receives a blank copy of the ASUP form above. One person is designated to keep track of the deliberations of the group using a laptop and the editable, fillable version of the ASUP that you'll also find on the Lives in the Balance website.

You should start with the Skills section. As a sidenote, we used to call them "lagging" skills, but that was problematic for members of the neurodivergent community, who felt that the word "lagging" has a neurotypical reference point and are understandably weary of having their differences viewed through a deficit lens. (We ought to listen to the neurodivergent community more often; they're among the most outspoken about the harms of punitive, exclusionary disciplinary practices, having been on the receiving end of more than their share of those practices.) So now it's just "skills." Completing the Skills section is fast (three to five minutes) and easy. No obsessing, no splitting of hairs, no head counts. Fast.

Another sidenote: there are many caregivers—a lot of them are educators—who have come to believe that all skills can be taught through direct instruction or a curriculum. While there are many skills that can be taught this way—reading, writing, math, spelling, entering a group, starting a conversation, and others—we have our doubts about whether the skills that are critical for adaptively handling problems and frustrations are best taught through a curriculum. Some skills are better taught through a *process*—through *experience*—than through a curriculum. What process is that? The process of solving problems collaboratively and proactively that you'll be reading about in chapter 5. So, while identifying skills provides more accurate, compassionate, and productive lenses through which to understand the child, these skills are not the primary targets of intervention; the unsolved problems are the targets of intervention. By engaging students in the process of solving problems collaboratively and proactively, you'll enhance the child's skills over time.

Then comes the hard(er) part, at least until you're good at it:

identifying unsolved problems. You'll see that there are prompts to help you get the ball rolling on identifying unsolved problems, and you'll want to go in order with the prompts (no prompt-hopping) and identify as many unsolved problems as possible for each prompt before moving on to the next prompt:

- Are there specific tasks or expectations the student is having difficulty completing or getting started on?
- Are there classmates this student has difficulty getting along with under certain conditions?
- Are there tasks and activities this student struggles to move from or to?
- Are there classes or activities the student has difficulty attending or being on time to?
- As you consider the start of the day to the end, are there any other expectations the student consistently has trouble meeting or that you find yourself frequently needing to remind them about?

The prompts get you in the ballpark on identifying and wording unsolved problems. The wording is important, because it's the wording of the unsolved problem on the ASUP that translates into the words that you're going to use when it comes time to introduce the unsolved problem to the student when you're about to start solving it together. Poorly worded unsolved problems often cause the entire problem-solving process to come to an unceremonious and abrupt stop before it even gets started (something we call *failure to launch*).

So, there are a few guidelines for the wording of unsolved problems. At the risk of having you get bogged down in the technicalities, the guidelines are described below. But there's also an excellent thirty-minute video on the Lives in the Balance website to teach you how to use the ASUP (www.livesinthebalance.org). There's also the ASUP Guide, which you'll find on the website as well. (By the way, all the resources on the website are free.)

Here are the guidelines; they'll make a lot more sense when you watch the video:

- **The wording of the unsolved problem should contain no concerning behaviors.** If you include the kid's concerning behavior in the wording of the unsolved problem, the student is likely to think they're in trouble, become defensive, and shut down. We don't want them to shut down; they have information we badly need. You're not talking with kids about their concerning behaviors anymore; you're talking with them about the problems that are causing those behaviors. So, all unsolved problems start with the word *Difficulty*, followed by a verb. Instead of writing, *"Gets upset and runs out of the room when trying to complete the double-digit division problems on the worksheet in math,"* you'd write, *"Difficulty completing the double-digit division problems on the worksheet in math."*
- **The wording of the unsolved problem contains no adult theories.** You wouldn't write, *"Difficulty using the software on the computer during math because she's adopted."* Just *"Difficulty using the software on the computer during math."* The theory (*because she's adopted*) is just a distraction, and there's an excellent chance it's wrong. As you'll see, you'll find out what's making it hard for the student to meet that expectation when you start trying to solve it collaboratively.
- **The wording of the unsolved problem is split, not clumped.** This is the hardest of the guidelines. You wouldn't write, *"Difficulty completing writing tasks during the school day,"* because that wording

isn't specific enough and refers to dozens of writing tasks, which assumes that the student is having difficulty on all writing tasks for the same reason (seldom will that be the case) and makes it hard for the student to respond. Instead, you'd write a separate unsolved problem for every writing task the student is having difficulty completing, for example, *"Difficulty writing the answers to the word problems in math,"* and *"Difficulty writing the lab reports in science."* In other words, in writing unsolved problems, you're focused on the micro, not the macro. (So common descriptors like "preferred" and "unpreferred" are out.) Is splitting going to make your list of unsolved problems longer? Yes, but it's going to greatly increase the likelihood that you get the information you're seeking. Can a long list of unsolved problems be overwhelming to caregivers who are now acutely aware, often for the first time, of the sheer number of expectations the student is having difficulty meeting? Yes, but it's even more overwhelming to have no idea what those unsolved problems are, thereby being relegated to focusing solely on the behaviors that are being caused by those unsolved problems.

Here are two strategies to help you split during an ASUP meeting:

- Ask "W" questions (who, what, where, when—but not why), for example, *"What assignments is the student having difficulty writing?"* or *"When are Michelle and Ashlee having difficulty getting along?"*
- Ask the question, *"What exactly is the expectation the child is struggling to meet?"*

All right, that's probably enough technicalities for now. We don't want to give them short shrift; it's extremely important to word those unsolved problems correctly. But we don't want to get bogged down in the technicalities here and, again, the video will make things really clear.

Light bulbs go on during ASUP meetings. It's often eye-opening for caregivers to learn that it's *skills* that are making it hard for a student to respond adaptively to problems and frustrations. And they're often blown away by the sheer number of expectations a student is having difficulty meeting across the course of the school day. This leads to some very important questions and productive responses:

- *"Wow. I didn't realize there were so many."* Good that we now realize there are so many.
- *"If I had this many unsolved problems, and I knew I was going to get whacked with them every time I showed up at school, I don't think I'd show up."* Some don't. *"I don't think I'd get out of bed."* Some don't.
- *"Can this student actually meet all of these expectations? And, if not, then why are we placing expectations on them that we already know they can't meet?"* These questions are going to help us think and do more about expectation management.
- *"Given how many expectations this student is having difficulty meeting, how much do we care about all of them? Do we care more about some than about others?"* These questions are going to help us prioritize, because we're not going to be able to solve all those problems at once, tempting though it might be to try.
- *"And this student only gets upset when these unsolved problems pop up?"* Roger that.
- *"And the unsolved problems aren't 'popping up' . . . we know they're coming!"* Roger that too.
- *"And if they're predictable, we can solve them proactively."* Yes, indeed.

That ASUP is a game changer. It's assessment gold.

What about all the other students? The ones who are doing reasonably well but still have some expectations that they're having difficulty meeting. For them (and you), there's the Early Problems Worksheet (EPW). It doesn't require a meeting and can be completed by an individual teacher. So, it's faster and easier. Why do we need it? Well, you might not, if identifying and solving problems with students is already your standard practice. But if you need something more formal to embed focusing on problems and solving them into your structures and practices you might want to use the Early Problems Worksheet so the problems (and the kids) don't get lost.

Early Problems Worksheet

Student's Name ____

Unsolved Problem ____

Date of Empathy Step ________________

What information was gathered from the student about what's making it hard for them to meet the above expectation?

What was the adult's concern (about how the unsolved problem is affecting the student and/or others)?

What solution was agreed upon?

Is the solution working, or is there a need to revisit the problem solving process?

What's Next?

Now you have an instrument (the ASUP) to help you change the conversation for the kids who aren't OK, moving from concerning behaviors, and theories, and diagnoses, to skills and unsolved problems. That is a major step in the direction of being early and meeting kids where they're at. And you have another instrument for all the other kids, all of whom struggle some of the time.

But you probably have some questions about how the ASUP fits into your existing structures for contemplating and providing supports and services to students who are struggling. We'll cover that in chapter 6. In the next chapter, we're going to be covering the problem-solving process to which we've been alluding.

Q & A

Question: Moving away from focusing on behaviors to the problems that are causing them is going to be a big shift, yes?

Answer: No question about it. But doing so will help your school take ten giant steps toward being early rather than late. And as you've read, doing so will help you appreciate the futility of a lot of the punitive, exclusionary disciplinary practices we've been busy applying to those behaviors.

Question: How is the ASUP really different from tools we already use, like FBAs and behavior rating scales?

Answer: FBAs and behavior checklists typically focus on defining and measuring *behavior*; the ASUP helps us identify the problems that are causing those behaviors. There's no need to wait for a behavior to occur before we recognize that a student is having difficulty meeting an expectation.

Question: Most FBAs I've read all came to the conclusion that a student's concerning behavior was for the purpose of *getting, escaping, and avoiding*. What are your thoughts on that?
Answer: As you've read, that's the traditional definition of the function of a kid's behavior. And if almost all FBAs say that, then we have serious doubts about the degree to which those FBAs set the stage for us to meet students where they're at. As you've read, concerning behaviors simply communicate that there are expectations a student is having difficulty meeting. That's a much more accurate, productive definition of "function." And a good FBA should be crystal clear about those unsolved problems and should point us in the direction of solving them.

Question: I've become jaded about meetings. I've sat through so many at my school . . . and obtained so little useful information about what I could do to help my students . . . they just feel like a waste of time.
Answer: We get it. You won't feel that way about ASUP meetings.

Question: What if I don't feel qualified to identify unsolved problems? I'm not a specialist.
Answer: You don't have to be. The unsolved problems have been there all along. They've been right in front of you. It's just a matter of focusing on them instead of on frustration responses.

Question: What if we don't have time to hold an ASUP meeting for every student?
Answer: As you've read, you won't be completing the ASUP for every student. The ASUP is for the students who are struggling the most, those we're already spending a great deal of time reacting to. All that reacting takes an enormous amount of time. Using the ASUP saves

time by reducing crisis management, repeated interventions, and staff frustration. For students with less intensive needs, the Early Problems Worksheet provides a faster way to track problems and solutions.

Closer Look: Consequences Are Late

By definition, a consequence is an event that occurs *after the fact*. That's late. A lot of people use the term "consequence" to refer to punishments, but the term can refer to either rewards or punishments. Lots of adults use rewards instead of punishments, but both are cut from the exact same bolt of cloth. Traditional school discipline has historically been based on modifying behavior through consequences. That's why the unsolved problems for the kids who aren't OK have piled up. Consequences aren't effective at solving problems because, as you've read, rewards and punishments aren't problem-solving strategies. So, while a suspension might give people a break from a kid, when the kid comes back to school all the unsolved problems that are causing the behaviors that people needed a break from are still there. Nothing has been accomplished, except that the kid has experienced another example of adults intervening in ways that aren't helpful and has received yet another reminder that school isn't for them.

This might be a good time to distinguish between natural consequences and adult-imposed consequences. Natural consequences are very powerful, very persuasive, and inevitable. If you touch the hot frying pan, you'll get burned. If you don't study for a test, you probably won't get a very good grade. If you don't share your toys with Billy, he probably won't want to play with you. The kids who aren't doing OK experience more natural consequences than most of us will in this lifetime. But what do a lot of adults think to do next when a kid's concerning behaviors (frustration responses) persist in the face of all those natural consequences? We add more, but those of the adult-imposed variety—detention, suspension, expulsion, being held in from recess, being held after school, loss of privileges, loss of stickers, corporal punishment—which are also very powerful and persuasive. But if those powerful, persuasive natural consequences didn't get the job done, there's really no reason to think that those of the adult-imposed variety will. None of the consequences solve any of the problems that are causing a student's frustration responses. None foster a safe school environment.

We should mention that the kids who aren't OK aren't the only ones who suffer in this scenario. The ones who are OK perpetually watch adults intervene in ways that are ineffective and counterproductive, continue to feel unsafe, and continue to have their learning disrupted. Those consequences aren't working for anyone.

....

"Better three hours too soon than a minute too late."
—William Shakespeare

"A problem well worded is a problem half-solved."
—Charles Kettering

5

Solving Problems Collaboratively

Earlier—this was in chapter 2—we talked about the developmental variability that typifies every classroom and the necessity of meeting every student where they're at. We also discussed the importance of accurately interpreting concerning behavior, focusing on unsolved problems rather than frustration responses, and being early rather than late (and you now have a technology for moving things in those directions). Finally, we talked about why it's so critical to be collaborative rather than unilateral in solving problems with students.

We're focusing on that last one in this chapter. If there are three things that typify many of the kids who aren't OK, it is these: (1) they've been on the receiving end of countless adult-imposed consequences; and (2) they've been on the receiving end of countless unilateral, adult-conceived interventions; and (3) they still have a lot of unsolved problems, telling us that numbers one and two didn't work. Those adult-conceived solutions often don't work because they leave someone very important out of the mix: the kid. That probably explains why *"Nothing about us without us"* has become a popular mantra among some members of the disability rights community.

It turns out that there are significant advantages to collaborating with kids on solving the problems that are affecting their lives. First, it's good for them to get practice solving problems. Second, they typically know more about what's making it hard for them to meet an expectation than adults might think (and what they know is often different from what adults were thinking). Third, they often come up with excellent solutions. Fourth, solutions that are arrived at with the involvement of the kid tend to save time, because those solutions tend to be way more effective and durable than those we adults generate without the kids' involvement.

The Plans

There are three options for handling an unsolved problem. They're called Plan A, Plan B, and Plan C.

Plan A involves solving a problem unilaterally. This is where adults are divining what's making it hard for a kid to meet an expectation and imposing a solution. If you've read the first four chapters, you know this is not the preferred, or even an especially productive, way of solving problems.

Plan B involves solving a problem collaboratively. This is where adults are partnering with a student to uncover what's making it hard for the student to meet an expectation and collaborating with the student on a solution. This is the preferred way of solving problems. It's also a good way to save a ton of time.

Plan C involves putting an expectation on hold, at least for now. Expectations that have been put on hold don't cause concerning behavior.

Though we're eager to tell you about Plan B, we're going to start with Plan C.

Plan C

There are three reasons you'd handle an expectation with Plan C.

Prioritizing: As you've read, students who have been struggling to meet expectations for a while typically have a lot of unsolved problems, many of them long-standing (we call those *old* unsolved problems). Trying to solve them all at once would be a guaranteed way to ensure that none get solved. Plus, some unsolved problems are more important than others. We're going to have to prioritize.

Stabilizing: There are some students who aren't going to be meeting any expectations because they're too unstable, volatile, and reactive. These students need us to be in stabilization mode, in which we are placing no expectations, or very few, on them except for coming to school. Every school needs a structure for stabilizing students. You're not going to get any educating done while the student is unstable. In other words, *there's no education without stabilization*. And there's no point in destabilizing them further with expectations they can't meet. Expectations that have been put on hold don't cause concerning behavior. These students can sometimes remain in their existing classroom; if that's not feasible, they can be placed in a special classroom that is created purely for stabilization purposes. Either way, they spend the school day doing largely preferred tasks, which gives the folks at school the opportunity to communicate with parents, outside mental health professionals, other service providers, and the folks doing the medicating to get all the ducks in a row on stabilization. That can take days, weeks, or months. Although this is a role that has often been played by inpatient units or outside placements—at great expense—we've often seen schools do a better job of stabilizing than those placements (once school personnel decide that stabilization is in their wheelhouse). As the student begins to stabilize, expectations can slowly be added back into the mix.

Expectation Management: Yes, this again. Apologies for the repetition (actually, we're not that sorry, since this is such an important concept), but the expectations that are particularly worthy of being put on hold are those that you believe are out of range for a student right now.

What does Plan C look like in a classroom? You're probably implementing some form of Plan C already (though it's unlikely you're calling it that). What you're doing is coming up with an *interim plan*—preferably in collaboration with the student—for what a student is going to be doing while an expectation is removed (and while the rest of the class is working on that expectation). Because we don't want the student wandering around the classroom interfering with the work of other students, better to come up with a proactive plan for what they'll be doing instead. While Plan C typically involves removing the expectation completely, it could mean the student is being expected to meet some modified, adapted, or adjusted form of the assignment *if you're certain they can.*

Here's what that conversation with the student could sound like:

Educator: *Anita, you know how we've been trying to solve some problems lately. We've been trying to figure out what's hard for you about the double-digit division problems on the worksheets in math. And we've been trying to figure out what's making it hard for you and Serena to get along on the school bus. And we've been trying to figure out what's been hard for you about getting to school on some days. We're working on a lot! I'm thinking that's plenty of things for us to be working on right now. So, I'm thinking that if we tried working on the difficulty you're having with the spelling words right now, it* *would be too much. How about me and you figure out what you're going to be doing while the rest of the class is working on their spelling words, and then we'll start focusing on the spelling words after we get some of the other problems solved.*

A tough part of Plan C for many educators is helping other students in the class understand why there are different expectations for different students. In other words, it's possible some students will need some help understanding the difference between *equity* and *equality* and why "fair" does not mean "equal." As you've read, equity means meeting every kid where they're at, which works out better for everyone. Equality means treating everyone exactly the same, meaning you're meeting no one where they're at. Of course, if you're differentiating instruction and personalizing learning, then the fact that different students are working on different things and in different ways is already established practice. But here's what it might sound like if a student missed the memo:

Student: *How come I have to do my science labs and Darius doesn't?*
Educator: *Because Darius is having difficulty on the science labs . . . and you're not.*
Student: *What if I start to have difficulty on the science labs?*
Educator: *Then I would help you with that. But are you having difficulty on the science labs?*
Student: *No.*
Educator: *I didn't think so. You don't usually have trouble with the science labs . . . you usually have difficulty writing the paragraphs in Writer's Workshop . . . that's why we're giving you the help you need with the paragraphs.*
Student: *So I have to do the science labs?*
Educator: *I'm having difficulty thinking of why you wouldn't.*

Naturally, this discussion would be most effective if it wasn't a one-shot deal. Helping students view the world through equity lenses, practicing it, talking the talk, and walking the walk, is a full-time endeavor and should be integral to the climate and culture of every classroom and school.

We appreciate the fact that equity has been a controversial topic lately, in politics anyway. While politicians may have the luxury of debating the value of equity, in schools, equity is an inescapable, acknowledged, appreciated, and celebrated way of life. As we discussed in chapter 2, given the developmental variability walking in the door, there's really no choice in the matter.

In students who have a lot of unsolved problems, a lot of those problems are going to be handled with Plan C initially. This can be challenging for educators who take pride in loading kids up with expectations. So just in case the thought of putting an expectation on hold for now makes you a bit queasy, remember this: *the student isn't meeting the expectation anyway*. So, you have two choices: (1) keep putting expectations on the student that you know they can't meet and cause concerning behavior (and all that goes along with it), or (2) make it official: the expectation is gone, for now. When will it come back? After you've solved some of your higher priority unsolved problems. You haven't given in, nor have you given up.

Plan B

OK, what about the problems you *are* actively trying to solve? That's where Plan B comes in. How many problems should you try to solve at any point in time? Never more than three, each separately. Otherwise, you're working on too many things at once. It took a long time for that pile of unsolved problems to accumulate; it's going to take a minute (or a few months) to chip away at them.

Which ones should you start solving first? Here's an algorithm to help you decide:

- **Safety:** Safety is a big deal in schools, so any unsolved problems setting in motion safety issues should be a very high priority.
- **Frequency:** If no unsolved problems are precipitating safety issues, you could prioritize the unsolved problems that are occurring most often.
- **Gravity:** The unsolved problems having the greatest negative impact on the student's life or the lives of others are worth prioritizing.

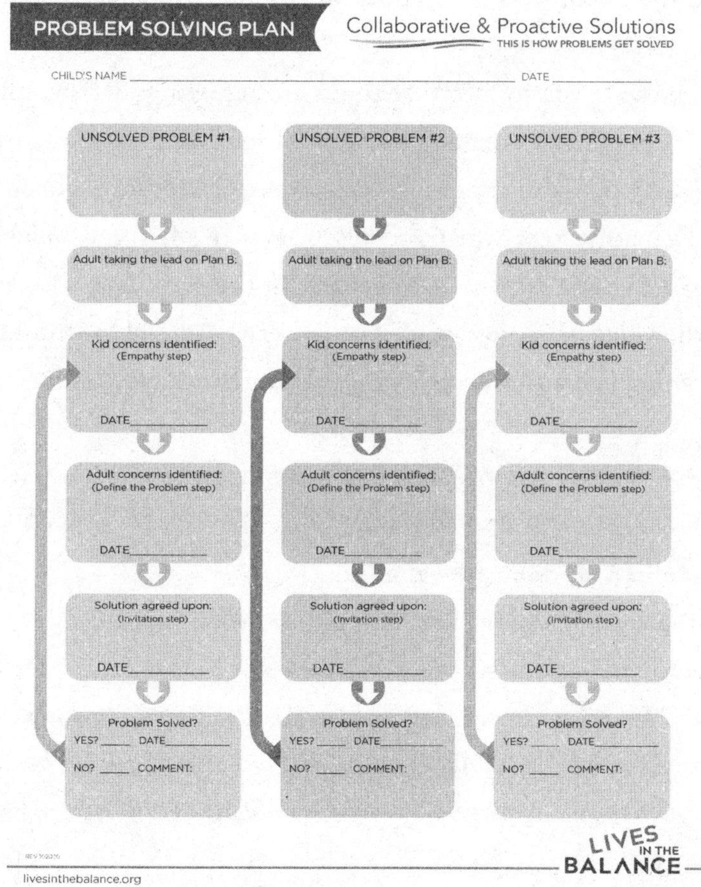

PROBLEM SOLVING PLAN

Collaborative & Proactive Solutions
THIS IS HOW PROBLEMS GET SOLVED

CHILD'S NAME ______ DATE ______

UNSOLVED PROBLEM #1	UNSOLVED PROBLEM #2	UNSOLVED PROBLEM #3
Adult taking the lead on Plan B:	Adult taking the lead on Plan B:	Adult taking the lead on Plan B:
Kid concerns identified: (Empathy step) DATE ______	Kid concerns identified: (Empathy step) DATE ______	Kid concerns identified: (Empathy step) DATE ______
Adult concerns identified: (Define the Problem step) DATE ______	Adult concerns identified: (Define the Problem step) DATE ______	Adult concerns identified: (Define the Problem step) DATE ______
Solution agreed upon: (Invitation step) DATE ______	Solution agreed upon: (Invitation step) DATE ______	Solution agreed upon: (Invitation step) DATE ______
Problem Solved? YES? ____ DATE ______ NO? ____ COMMENT:	Problem Solved? YES? ____ DATE ______ NO? ____ COMMENT:	Problem Solved? YES? ____ DATE ______ NO? ____ COMMENT:

livesinthebalance.org

LIVES IN THE BALANCE

Just in case you're inclined to obsess over which problems to start solving first, don't. It's more important to get started on solving problems than it is to decide which ones to prioritize.

How do you keep track of the problems you're solving and your progress in solving them? With the second sheet of the CPS model, the Problem Solving Plan, also available in an editable/fillable format on the Lives in the Balance website (www.livesinthebalance.org).

Plan B involves three steps: the Empathy step, the Define Adult Concerns step, and the Invitation step. We could spend many pages telling you about the technicalities and nuances of the process. But we're going to stick to the most important points about each step and save the technicalities and nuances for the videos that accompany this book on the website.

It is in the Empathy step that adults are gathering information from a student about what's making it hard for the student to meet a particular expectation. We always warn caregivers to be prepared for surprises in the Empathy step, when you discover that what you *thought* was getting in the way is *not* what's getting in the way. This will come to life in the videos, but, just to give you a very basic feel for things when they're going fast and smoothly, here's how that might sound:

Teacher: *I've noticed you've been having difficulty following along as I read* All American Boy *to the class. What's up?*

Middle School Student: *No point.*

Teacher: *So, you're saying there's no point in following along?*

Student: *That's right.*

Teacher: *Help me understand why you feel there's no point in following along.*

Student: *Remember those days I was absent last week? I fell behind on the story, so now there's no point in my following along. So I just go to sleep.*

Again, that was super-fast and seamless; we just want to give you a feel for things before you watch videos of Plan B. Notice we're not talking about the student's concerning behavior (going to sleep in class), we're talking about the unsolved problem that precedes it.

In the Define Adult Concerns step, the adult is entering their concern into consideration. The very same concern that might previously have prompted a unilateral solution is now being addressed collaboratively. Adult concerns are the answer to the question: *Why is it important that this expectation be met?* Many adults have never given that question much thought. There are basically two possibilities: (1) because of how the unsolved problem is affecting the student and/or (2) because of how the unsolved problem is affecting other people. And within those two categories, the concerns are almost always about health, safety, and/or learning (and sometimes fairness). Here's how that would sound on the same unsolved problem but, again, quite seamless:

Teacher: *My concern is that if you don't follow along, you won't get practice at answering questions after you hear or read a story. And that's something a lot of assignments require you to do.*

In the Invitation step, student and educator are putting their heads together and collaborating on a solution. The solution needs to be *realistic* (meaning both parties can truly do what they're agreeing to do) and *mutually satisfactory* (meaning the solution truly addresses the concerns of both parties). If those two criteria aren't met, it's highly unlikely that the solution will work. Here's what a super-fast, seamless Invitation step would sound like, again, just to give you a feel for things:

Teacher: *So, I wonder if there's a way for us to get you caught up on the story (the kid's concern) and also make sure you get practice at answering questions after you read or listen to a story. Do you have any ideas?*

That's right, you're giving the student the first crack at the solution. Not because they alone are on the hook for coming up with a solution, but because you want to give the kid practice at coming up with realistic and mutually satisfactory solutions.

Student: *Could you meet with me sometime to get me caught up on the story? Then there would be a good reason for me to follow along.*
Teacher: *I could do that. Maybe during study hall today?*
Student: *That works.*
Teacher: *Here I was thinking you just didn't like the story.*
Student: *No, I like the story.*

Those are the basics. You'll be reading some additional Plan B dialogues in subsequent chapters, and chapter 7 is devoted to answering some common questions about Plan B, but we can't wait for you to watch the videos of Plan B that accompany this book so you can see and hear those steps and gain an appreciation for the nuances and what to do when things don't go so seamlessly. Again, you can find those videos at www.livesinthebalance.org.

You might be thinking, We talk with kids all the time in our school. Perhaps so, but let's consider why Plan B conversations are quite different and far more productive. First, often conversations with kids who are struggling are focused on their frustration responses rather than the unsolved problems that are causing them.

With Plan B, you're talking about the unsolved problems, not the concerning behavior:

- **Not this:** *I saw you hit Billy on the playground while you guys were playing foursquare. Can you think of what you should have done instead?*
- **This:** *I've noticed that you and Billy are having difficulty agreeing on the rules of the foursquare game during recess. What's up?*

Also, in many conversations we have with kids, the topic is often quite broad; as you learned in chapter 4, the unsolved problems you're talking with kids about in this process are quite specific.

- **Not this:** *I've noticed you're having difficulty doing work at school.*
- **This:** *I've noticed you're having difficulty completing the double-digit division problems on the worksheet in math.*

In many typical conversations adults have with kids, we're telling the kid why *we* think they're struggling and what *we've* decided will be done about it. When you're doing Plan B, you've put your theories and your unilateral solutions on the shelf.

- **Not this:** *I've noticed you're having difficulty getting to school on time because you really don't want to be here. What can we do so you want to be here more?*
- **This:** *I've noticed you're having difficulty getting to school on time. What's up?*

And many conversations adults have with kids take place reactively, in the heat of the moment, often when an unsolved problem has "popped up" yet again. Now you know that unsolved problems don't "pop up," and that waiting for frustration responses is bad timing for just about everything (unless you're selling crisis management programs). Thanks to the ASUP and Problem Solving Plan, 99 percent of your Plan B conversations should be proactive. You're not waiting for frustration responses anymore.

As we mentioned earlier, there are a lot of skills being practiced and enhanced when a student is participating in Plan B. In the Empathy step, the student is learning how to figure out and articulate what's been getting in their way and is being heard. Critical skill. The adults are listening (the purest form of empathy), hearing, understanding, and taking the kid's perspective. Indispensable. In the Define Adult Concerns step, kids are learning to listen (not listening to respond, listening to understand), to take another person's perspective and appreciate how their actions are affecting others. Huge. In the Invitation step, both kid and adult are getting good at generating alternative solutions, resolving disagreements without conflict, and coming up with solutions that address not only one's own concerns but also the concerns of someone else. Massive. Adults are modeling all those skills and, as a bonus, maybe getting some practice themselves. Exactly what the kids who aren't OK need. Exactly what every kid needs.

Best of all, problems that have gone unsolved for a very long time are being solved. Concerning behavior is dramatically reduced (because, as you know, it's only unsolved problems that cause concerning behavior; *solved* problems don't). The need for punitive, exclusionary discipline and de-escalating, restraining, and secluding kids is dramatically reduced and, over time, probably eliminated. You didn't want to be doing those things anyway.

Plan A

Do you still need Plan A? Maybe in extreme, surprising situations involving safety. Beyond that, there are only disadvantages to solving problems using Plan A. Imposing solutions on kids *heightens* the likelihood of frustration responses. That's because most of us (kids included) don't love having solutions imposed. Plan A also involves power, and power causes conflict. If we're using Plan A, *we never find out what's making it hard for a student to meet a particular expectation* . . . because we never ask. That's why we refer to solutions arrived at through use of Plan A as *uninformed.* While it might seem that Plan A is efficient, one failed solution after another is actually quite time-consuming. In other words, problems that seem solved through use of Plan A are usually only temporarily solved. Which means they really aren't solved at all.

The kids who aren't OK don't need more Plan A. They've had more than their share. Being responsive to developmental variability, meeting kids where they're at, helping all students feel they belong, giving them hope, and ensuring that they receive the supports they need has a lot more to do with Plans B and C.

And all students—including the ones who are doing OK—learn that collaboration, rather than power, is the best way to solve problems durably; how to work together toward solutions that are realistic and mutually satisfactory; and how to listen to one another's concerns rather than simply offer up solutions.

Q & A

Question: At what tier is all this problem-solving taking place?

Answer: Any tier. Every tier. With or without tiers. The earlier the better.

Question: Isn't Plan B mostly for special education students?
Answer: No, it's for any student who is struggling to meet an expectation, with or without an IEP.

Question: Are antecedent interventions—modifying the environment to make it less aversive, changing task demands to make them easier, shorter, less aversive, and incorporating student interest and preferences—Plan A?
Answer: If those interventions are implemented without any information from a student about what's making it hard for them to meet an expectation, and without any student involvement in generating and finalizing the solution, then, yes, those interventions are Plan A.

Question: Goodness, a *lot* of interventions that are applied to students—strategies, accommodations, plugging them into services—are based on little or no input from the students themselves! Thoughts?
Answer: We shouldn't be surprised when those interventions don't work. Most of the solutions arrived at through Plan B have little or nothing to do with modifying or adapting expectations, making accommodations, or plugging kids into services. And, as with antecedent interventions, if we're modifying or adapting expectations, making accommodations, or plugging kids into services without knowing what's really getting in the way of meeting an expectation and without input and sign-off from the student, then we're just guessing . . . and also using Plan A.

Question: And you think we have time to do Plan B?
Answer: Again, possibly not, at least not as things are currently configured in your building. There's no question that the school schedule wasn't designed to give educators time to solve problems with

kids (apparently, the schedule was constructed without giving thought to the fact that some students were going to have difficulty meeting our expectations). And the school discipline program was designed to make it easy to send those kids to someone else, either the principal or assistant principal (for discipline) or the school psychologist or school counselor (for counseling). The fact that unsolved problems have piled up is an indication of the shortcomings of such designs. So, we have some re-designing to do. We're going to have to create structures that create time. That requires commitment more than anything else. It's not that hard.

The reality is we're already spending significant time reacting to concerning behavior. The goal is to shift that time from reactive to proactive by solving the problems that are causing those very time-consuming behaviors. One fifteen-minute Plan B can prevent multiple classroom interruptions, saving far more time in the long run. Starting with just one or two students can free up instructional minutes and emotional energy, making classrooms calmer and more productive. Plan B takes time . . . but it gives a lot more back.

Question: I need to ask again. You're sure you're not trying to turn educators into therapists?
Answer: Positive. Again, as an educator, you've always been a problem-solver. But because we've also seen the limits of unilateral, reactive problem-solving, we need to help you become a *collaborative, proactive* problem-solver. That's going to require some new skills and some new structures.

Question: Early in my teaching career, I always went to the student first to find out what was making it hard for them to meet an expectation. Now we rush into deciding what tier a student is in, get the behavior intervention plan done quickly, and the student's voice has been lost. No wonder I'm so unhappy!

Answer: Nothing particularly rewarding in thinking about tiers, getting a behavior plan done quickly, and being unilateral. Nothing rewarding about adhering to an algorithm for responding to concerning behaviors without solving the problems that are causing them. It isn't just students who've paid the price for these developments, educators have paid a heavy price too.

Question: I tried Plan B a few times before, and my students talked, but I got stuck because I didn't know what to say after they said something.

Answer: There are eight drilling strategies to help you know what to say to probe further, and you'll find descriptions of them on the Drilling Cheat Sheet on the Lives in the Balance website. Drilling strategies help kids clarify what's making it hard for students to meet an expectation; they help kids know that you're listening to and trying to understand them. The three you'll be using the most are *reflective listening* (simply saying back to the student whatever they just said to you); *asking W questions* (who, what, where, when—we tend to stay away from why); and *summarizing and asking for more* (recapping the concerns you've heard so far in the Empathy step and asking if there are any others.) You'll see the drilling strategies come to life in the videos we've been recommending you watch.

Question: What if I'm bad at Plan B?

Answer: Since it's a new skill for many adults, you might not be great at Plan B in the beginning. You'll be fine. You just need some passion, persistence, and problem-solving. But mostly some practice.

Question: So, with Plan C I'm basically doing nothing?
Answer: No. Prioritizing, stabilizing, and expectation management aren't nothing; they are a big deal.

Question: Plan C sounds to me like lowering expectations. Aren't we supposed to believe all kids can succeed?
Answer: Plan C is not about lowering expectations. Every student is their own reference point. Every student still has a path toward growth, but just like a physical therapy plan adapts to where your knee is today, your teaching adapts to where a child is right now. Meeting a student where they're at isn't giving up on them; it's the most hopeful, respectful, and equity-driven thing we can do.

Question: Look, some students just aren't motivated. I've tried everything, and they don't care. Why will this work?
Answer: It's very frustrating to use every tool in your toolbox and have little to show for it. Plan B works because it isn't focused on a student's behavior, isn't dependent on adult theories about what's making it hard for a kid to meet an expectation, isn't dependent on adult solution repertoires, and engages kids in the process of solving the problems that are affecting their lives at school. Those ingredients have probably been missing from what you've done already. When we shift from asking "How do I motivate this student?" to "What's getting in their way?," we move toward problem-solving, not power struggles.

Closer Look: What Counts

Given how keen we are on counting behaviors in schools these days—often to gauge a student's progress—what do we do if we're mandated to quantify a student's progress (or lack thereof) but want to move away from counting frustration responses? Well, since pretty much *everything* can be quantified, you could instead quantify unsolved problems and the degree to which they've been solved. Just create a scale and start quantifying! Here's an example:

Sample Unsolved Problem: Difficulty getting started on the Ponce de Leon social studies project.

5 = able to meet the expectation reliably

4 = mostly able to meet the expectation

3 = still having difficulty meeting the expectation sometimes

2 = still having difficulty meeting the expectation most of the time

1 = always having difficulty meeting the expectation

Why have we been so busy counting and quantifying frustration responses? We didn't realize there was something else—something much more important—to count and quantify. Much better to count and quantify what's early rather than what's late.

....

"Not all things worth counting are countable and not all things that count are worth counting."

—Albert Einstein

6

Putting the Horse Back in Front of the Cart

We've covered a lot of territory in five chapters. Because a lot of what you've read isn't conventional wisdom, we're thinking it might be a good idea to review the key points thus far:

- Many of the changes that have occurred over the past two decades have worked to the disadvantage of kids. While it's good for educators to be sensitive to these changes, and their impact on kids, they can't address most of them directly.
- What educators can do is create school and classroom ecosystems that are responsive to the *developmental variability* of their students, with every student as their own reference point.
- The definition of good teaching is *meeting every student where they're at.* The quality of a school is determined by the degree to which it meets that definition. High-stakes testing has made it harder for educators and schools to meet that definition.
- Concerning behavior is a student's frustration or distress response, which occurs when a student is having difficulty meeting an expectation. We refer to those unmet expectations as *unsolved problems.*
- Frustration responses can be lucky or unlucky. A mountain of research indicates that students with unlucky frustration responses

are struggling with important skills, such as flexibility/adaptability, frustration tolerance, problem-solving, and emotion regulation. There is no research indicating that unlucky frustration responses are due to poor motivation. Students with unlucky frustration responses are often on the receiving end of the most harsh, punitive discipline schools have to offer.

- *Expectation management* refers to ensuring that the expectations that are being placed on a student are those the student can actually meet. There are a variety of pressures that have caused educators to feel the need to place expectations on students that they can't meet. Doing so simply causes frustration responses.
- De-escalating, restraining, and secluding kids, punitive/exclusionary discipline, and a whole host of common practices in schools are late, reactive, downstream interventions. They occur well after an unsolved problem has set in motion concerning behavior. They do more harm than good. And they do not solve any of the problems that are causing those behaviors. With so many kids who are struggling, anything you can do to head upstream—to get out in front of those unsolved problems—will be critical. The absolute last thing you'd want to be is late.
- The Assessment of Skills and Unsolved Problems (ASUP) helps educators focus on unsolved problems rather than behaviors. Since unsolved problems are early (upstream) and concerning behaviors are late (downstream), the ASUP is a major step forward in creating structures that are proactive rather than reactive. You don't need to complete the ASUP for every student; just the ones who are struggling the most. Focusing on unsolved problems also helps us be more responsive to the developmental variability inherent in every classroom and meet every student where they're at.

- Plan B involves solving problems collaboratively—meaning with the full involvement of the student—and proactively. The information gathered in Plan B should go a long way toward informing discussions about services and supports that might be helpful to a student.
- Plan C helps us prioritize (because you can't solve everything at once), stabilize (because stabilization comes before education), and ensure that our expectations are well-matched to individual students (because placing expectations on students that we already know they can't meet makes no sense and only causes frustration responses).

How do we integrate these new tools, targets, information, and points of emphasis into our existing structures for helping the kids who aren't OK? Are those existing structures serving those students well? Do those structures need to be changed? Here we go.

Triage

With so many students who are struggling, the first thing we need is a system for identifying the kids who are struggling the most and who need help most urgently. In emergency rooms and urgent care clinics, they organize their efforts by triaging. Patients with heart attack or stroke symptoms, altered mental status, and head injuries are seen and treated urgently. Patients with coughs, runny noses, constipation, diarrhea, and rashes tend to wait.

How do schools triage? Tiers. And special education. Which, as it relates to putting the horse in front of the cart, is bass ackwards.

For the unfamiliar, systems such as multi-tiered systems of support (MTSS) are general education *organizational* structures that essentially designate *who's doing what.* Tier 1 includes supports and practices that are being provided to all students and can include additional supports that are provided by the classroom teacher for students for whom existing practices and supports are insufficient. Tier 1 is also where we're making sure that our expectations for students are crystal clear and where we're examining whether best practices are being applied. Tier 2 kicks in when it's clear a student needs additional supports (inside or outside of the classroom) beyond those provided by the classroom teacher. And Tier 3 signifies that even more intensive intervention is needed (often outside of the classroom) by staff besides the classroom teacher. School systems vary widely in the supports they offer and equally widely on the supports that are pegged to each of the three tiers.

Figuring out who's doing what (and where it's being done) is, of course, a necessity. But, as noted in chapter 4, *you can't figure out who's doing what for a student until you determine what that student needs*. And it's equally critical that determining what a student needs not be robotic, formulaic, based exclusively on adult theories, or focused heavily on a student's concerning behavior. So, it's absolutely essential to complete the ASUP and gather information from the student about what's making it hard for them to meet expectations *way before* talking about the tiers.

As an important sidenote, the precursor to MTSS is another tiered system, Positive Behavioral Interventions and Supports (PBIS). The B in PBIS tells you something very important: the intervention ingredients of PBIS are focused on behaviors (and modifying them). That being the case, we think the tiers of PBIS simply provide an organizational layer for heading downstream. (Be sure to read about the evidence base for PBIS, and lots of other models, in chapter 10.) PBIS isn't focused on unsolved problems and gathering information from students about what's making it hard for them to meet certain expectations. And—this can be a little confusing—while PBIS is said to focus on behavioral *skills*, those "skills" are actually discrete *behaviors*. What educators are trained to do in PBIS is teach and reteach replacement behaviors and check-in and check-out about them.

Another system for deciding who's doing what is special education. In the U.S., determining whether a student qualifies for special education involves the fairly lengthy process of establishing whether the student has one or more of thirteen disabilities, including autism, emotional and/or behavioral disability, other health impairment (including ADHD), developmental disability, specific learning disability, intellectual impairment, intellectual disability, speech and language disability, deafblind, visual impairment, hearing impairment, orthopedic or physical impairment, and traumatic brain injury. The disability must cause impairment that is significant enough to impact the child's learning or behavior at school and must require specialized instruction.

While special education is a wonderful thing if a student needs something it offers, many discussions about students who are struggling are focused rather narrowly on the question of whether the student has a disability that qualifies. In many schools, that question takes a back seat to determining what a student actually needs. This could be viewed, once again, as the cart leading the horse. The ASUP and gathering information about what's making it hard for a student to meet expectations should come *before* determining whether a student needs something special education has to offer. As you've read, the ASUP should be the standard pre-referral, triage instrument in every school.

So how should we be triaging instead? *Based on a student's level of acuity.*

We're not big on categorizing kids, but there are some students—we could refer to them as *high-support needs*—who receive all or most of their instruction and supports outside of a general education classroom. While we believe that it is possible (more possible than many think) to involve these students in the process of solving the problems that are affecting their lives, plugging those students into services tends to be more straightforward.

The second category of students are the kids who have *many* unsolved problems. They may also have unlucky frustration responses that are dangerous and disruptive. And they often have difficulties that go well beyond what their classroom teacher will be able to provide. We might call these our *High Acuity* students. Because their unsolved problems and frustration responses have typically been in place for a long time, those students are often already receiving MTSS supports and special education services. And yet, they're still struggling. The fact that they're still not doing well is typically an indication that, whatever supports and services have been provided thus far, at whatever tier and with or without special education services, *we're still not meeting them where they're at.* Almost always, *their unsolved problems have yet to be identified and solved.*

First and foremost, what do those students need? They need the ASUP, ASAP. Then they need us to move into expectation management mode, prioritize their unsolved problems, start solving the high-priority problems, and putting the rest on hold.

In many school systems, there is a six-week Tier 1 waiting period before a more intensive level of intervention is considered. Those six weeks are spent with the classroom teacher doing their level best to help the student. If things don't go well—and as evidenced by the long waiting lists to get the Tier 2 ball rolling, they often don't—then those six weeks of waiting aren't fair to the student or their teacher. Because High Acuity students have many unsolved problems, may have frustration responses that are dangerous and disruptive, and may clearly have needs that go well beyond what their classroom teacher will be able to provide, it makes no sense—for anyone—to wait six weeks.

The third category of students have less acute needs. They have a more manageable number of unsolved problems, their frustration responses are not dangerous or significantly disruptive, and the classroom teacher feels that the student's needs can be reasonably met in the classroom.

We could call them *Low Acuity* students. Does it make sense to allow the teacher time to try to get a handle on these students' difficulties and tap into their repertoire of hypotheses and interventions? Sure. But, even for these students, the clock is ticking. If the first few "unassisted interventions"—interventions teachers divine—don't work, it's time to stop divining and start engaging the student in Plan B.

Low Acuity students are still at risk. If their problems don't get identified and solved, they start to exhibit bigger frustration responses, and if those frustration responses are handled with traditional consequence-based school discipline, they'll become High Acuity students soon enough. And by the time they're High Acuity students, we're late again. (If you can't decide whether the student is High Acuity or Low Acuity, default to the former.)

Finally, there are all the other students; the ones who are meeting most expectations and only have intermittent unsolved problems. It's just as important that we rapidly notice when they're having difficulty meeting an expectation and that we engage them in the process of solving that problem.

Is it OK to give the students in the third and fourth categories the chance to surmount unsolved problems on their own? Sure, over the course of a few days. Waiting longer than that only increases the likelihood of frustration responses (and we definitely don't want to be in the habit of noticing that a student is having difficulty meeting an expectation only if they exhibit concerning behavior).

Supports and Services: A Pool of Help

All right, now we have a system to identify the students who need our help most urgently. Let's think about the existing structures through which we organize the help students receive and whether those structures are working well for the kids who aren't OK and their teachers.

Whether it's MTSS or special education, we think it's best to conceive of the array of supports and services that can be offered to a student as existing within a large "pool." Those supports and services and their quality vary widely across schools and school systems. In special education, those supports and services—and we're not being exhaustive here—can include things like occupational therapy, physical therapy, speech and language therapy, executive skills coaching, social skills coaching, reading remediation, assistive technology support, academic intervention and tutoring, peer mentoring and buddy programs, and alternative and augmentative communication (AAC) support.

As things currently stand, in the middle of the pool is a metaphorical safety divider separating services that are available to all students in general education (we could call that the shallow end, or MTSS supports) and services that are only available through special education (the deep end). With all due respect to those who strive to protect the integrity of the process of determining whether a student qualifies for special education, most High Acuity students are pretty much *guaranteed* to qualify for having a disability. That's because they're highly likely to fall into one or more of at least three of the thirteen disability categories under the Individuals with Disabilities Education Act (IDEA): autism, other health impairment, and emotional disturbance. So *qualifying* isn't generally the biggest issue.

Figuring out what supports and services a student needs from the pool—whether what they need is in the deep end or the shallow end, or both—*is* the biggest issue. We can't make that determination until we've identified a student's unsolved problems and gathered information from them about what's making it hard for them to meet certain expectations. Doing so helps move us away from a largely adult-driven process that places kids in buckets based on eligibility requirements and toward a process that is driven by engaging students in the process of determining where they're at so we can meet them there. Thus, the critical questions we should really be trying to answer are: *Given what we now know about what's making it hard for the student to meet certain expectations—based heavily, but not exclusively, on information we've gathered from the student—do they need a service or support that's in the deep end of the pool? And given all the time, effort, and discussion that is devoted to it, is the deep end and shallow end arrangement really the best way to organize things?* We'll answer the second question first: no. The kids who aren't OK—and their educators—need flexibility way more than they need rigid, onerous structures governing what they get.

Let's think about what the answer to the first question could look like, starting with our High Acuity students. As you know, these are the students that schools struggle with the most. They have a lot of unsolved problems, tend to have unlucky frustration responses, may have poor attendance (often a by-product of years and years of having problems go unsolved and being on the receiving end of punitive, exclusionary discipline), and may already carry multiple psychiatric diagnoses. You could make a list of the High Acuity students in your school in two minutes. As we've noted, there's a high probability they're already receiving special education services. All those services, diagnoses, IEPs, FBAs, behavior plans, all that time, and they're still not doing well. What would it look like if we began involving the kid in the process of determining what's getting in the way for them and what they need from us?

1. Do the ASUP, ASAP. Determine whether a student's level of acuity is so off the charts that the top priority is stabilization. While that scenario should apply to very few students, it's

a critical first consideration. As you've read, when you're in stabilization mode, almost all expectations will be removed until the student is able to start working on some expectations. Stabilization comes before education.

2. Prioritize which problems are to be solved and which are to be put on hold for now.
3. Determine whether it's feasible for the student to remain in the general ed classroom while staff are busy with the task of using Plan B for some unsolved problems and Plan C for the rest. If it's feasible, that's probably Tier 1 (if that really matters anymore). If it's not feasible, decisions need to be made about where the student will be placed (and that's probably Tier 2 or 3, for those still keeping track of that).
4. Given what you've learned from the student about what's making it hard for them to meet certain expectations, what other services might the school or school system have to offer, beyond solving problems collaboratively?

If you're a visual person, here's the same information depicted graphically:

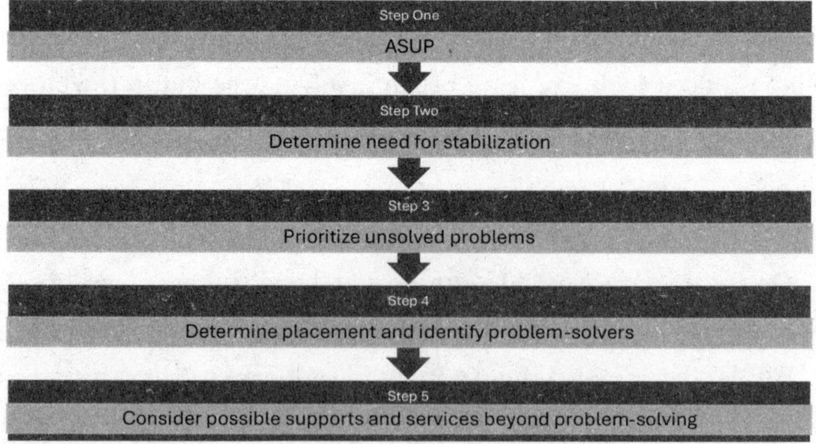

How would the above blueprint play out with our friend Jackson from chapter 3? First, recall that Jackson was already placed in a special education classroom. Because it's already recognized that he has a lot of unsolved problems and that his frustration responses can be unlucky, he's a High Acuity student. But the ASUP has never been completed for Jackson, so his unsolved problems have never been formally identified or prioritized. In keeping with the blueprint, the ASUP would be completed first (Step One). See on the opposite page what Jackson's completed ASUP looked like. As you'll see, his teacher, paraprofessional, ed tech, and school psychologist checked off almost every skill and identified twenty-four different unsolved problems, including expectations they had already removed but were hopeful that Jackson might meet at some point.

The group decided that Jackson was not in need of a special arrangement for stabilization purposes (Step Two). Then they identified the three unsolved problems they intended to solve first (Step Three). The unsolved problems that were causing safety issues were identified as their top priorities:

- Difficulty completing the division problems on the worksheet in math
- Difficulty getting along with Dante during recess
- Difficulty coming back into the classroom after recess

The remaining unsolved problems were placed on hold (Plan C). The group decided that Jackson's unsolved problems could be solved by staff in his special education classroom (Step 4). They made no decisions about whether extra or different supports were needed for Jackson for the problems they had prioritized (Step 5), as they hadn't yet determined, through Plan B, what was making it hard for Jackson to meet those expectations.

ASUP 2024
ASSESSMENT OF SKILLS AND UNSOLVED PROBLEMS

Collaborative & Proactive Solutions
THIS IS HOW PROBLEMS GET SOLVED

CHILD'S NAME: **Jackson** DATE:

NAMES OF CAREGIVERS COMPLETING THIS INSTRUMENT:

STEP 1: SKILLS

Whether neurotypical or neurodivergent, children communicate that they're having difficulty meeting expectations in diverse ways, including through their concerning behavior. This behavior is best conceived as a frustration or stress response, the nature of which is determined by a variety of factors, most especially certain skills related to flexibility/adaptability, frustration tolerance, problem solving, and emotion regulation. Some kids can demonstrate these skills under some conditions but not under other conditions.

This section is aimed at helping caregivers discuss those skills and the degree to which they may be impacting a particular child. Being aware of and considering the skills that may impact a child's capacity to handle life's problems and frustrations and meet various expectations helps caregivers move away from motivational explanations for concerning behavior (e.g. attention-seeking, manipulative, coercive, unmotivated) and toward a more compassionate, accurate understanding of such behavior. Note that these skills are not the primary focal point of intervention in the CPS model; the unsolved problems you'll be identifying in Step 2 will be the "targets" of intervention.

Please check off a skill if it's difficult for the child to access at times and appears to be making it difficult for the child to handle problems and frustrations and/or meet certain expectations:

- ✔ Maintain focus
- ✔ Regulate activity level
- ✔ Handle transitions, shift from one mindset to another
- ✔ Consider the likely outcomes or consequences of actions (impulse control)
- ✔ Persist on challenging or tedious tasks
- Sense of time (time that has passed, time needed)
- ✔ Consider a range of solutions to problems
- ✔ Flexibly handle ambiguity, uncertainty
- ✔ Shift from original idea, plan, or solution
- Express concerns, needs, or thoughts in words or other means of communication
- Understand what is being communicated by others
- ✔ Appreciate how their actions affect others
- ✔ Regulate emotional response to problems and frustrations
- ✔ Empathize with others, appreciate another person's perspective or point of view
- Interoception (ability to understand and feel what's going on inside their body)
- Tolerate and manage the sensory environment

STEP 2: UNSOLVED PROBLEMS

Unsolved problems are the specific expectations a child is having difficulty meeting. The wording of an unsolved problem will translate directly into the words that you'll be using when you introduce the unsolved problem to the child when it comes time to solve the problem together. Poorly worded unsolved problems often cause the problem-solving process to deteriorate before it even gets started. Please reference the ASUP Guide for guidance on writing unsolved problems.

SCHOOL/FACILITY PROMPTS

- Are there specific tasks/expectations the student is having difficulty completing or getting started on?
- Are there classmates this student is having difficulty getting along with in specific conditions?
- Are there tasks and activities this student is having difficulty moving from or to?
- Are there classes/activities the student is having difficulty attending/being on time to?
- As you think about the start of the day to the end, are there any other expectations the student has difficulty reliably meeting or that you find yourself frequently reminding the child about?

HOME/CLINIC PROMPTS

- Are there chores/tasks/activities the child is having difficulty completing or getting started on?
- Are there siblings/other children the child is having difficulty getting along with in specific conditions?
- Are there aspects of hygiene the child is having difficulty completing?
- Are there activities the child is having difficulty ending or tasks the child is having difficulty moving on to?
- As you think about the start of the day to the end, are there any other expectations the child has difficulty reliably meeting or that you find yourself frequently reminding the child about?

List unsolved problems here:
(or on a separate sheet)

Difficulty starting the Do Now first thing in the morning
Difficulty coming straight to the classroom after getting off the bus
Difficulty getting along with Sam on the school bus
Difficulty keeping hands to self on the school bus
Difficulty completing double-digit division problems on math worksheet
Difficulty writing paragraphs in Writer's Workshop
Difficulty keeping hands to self in line to recess
Difficulty keeping hands to self in line to lunch
Difficulty keeping hands to self in bus line
Difficulty coming back into the classroom after recess
Difficulty going to Ms. Taylor's office
Difficulty speaking kindly to Caleb during social skills group
Difficulty getting along with Amir during lunch
Difficulty sitting next to Candace during morning meeting
Difficulty remaining quiet while other students are speaking during morning meeting
Difficulty asking permission to use the restroom
Difficulty speaking kindly to Jerod if Jerod makes a mistake in reading group
Difficulty moving from choice time to Writer's Workshop
Difficulty moving from choice time to ELA
Difficulty being on time to catch the school bus at 7:35
Difficulty completing spelling worksheet
Difficulty packing up backpack at the end of the day

LIVESINTHEBALANCE.ORG

LIVES IN THE BALANCE

Then they started solving problems with Jackson. Let's revisit the scenario you read about in chapter 3 and see how things could have turned out differently once the problem-solving process took place:

Jackson came in from recess after having played foursquare with his former adversary, Dante. It turned out that Dante and Jackson had very different notions of the rules of foursquare, but their teacher had helped them sort that out and come up with a solution, and the foursquare game was no longer causing conflict between the two kids.

The paraprofessional put a math worksheet in front of Jackson and told him she'd be back to help him with it.

Jackson took a quick glance at the worksheet and promptly announced, to now one in particular, "I'm not doing it."

"Jackson, hold tight, I'll be right back," said the para.

Jackson slouched at his desk until the para returned.

"What's up, bud?"

"I'm hot."

"Ah, right, you're frequently hot when you come in from recess and that makes it hard for you to get down to work on your math worksheets right away. We talked about that. So, remember what we decided the solution should be?"

"Oh, yeah," said Jackson, now rising out of his seat to work at a computer station.

"How long do you think it will take you to cool off today?" asked the para.

"Five minutes?" Jackson estimated.

"See you soon."

"Do I have to do math when I come back?"

"Yeah, remember we talked about that too. You told me the math worksheets were hard for you to read, so I was going to read the paragraphs to you and then I'd help you with the math if you needed it."

"Oh, yeah," said Jackson, settling in front of the computer to play a math game. "Be there soon."

Is everything going to be copasetic with Jackson now that two problems have been solved? Hard to imagine. There are a lot more problems to be solved, so there's still quite the pile remaining. But they're on their way.

Are they going to have to do Plan B on all twenty-four unsolved problems? Not a chance; some are going to be solved by solving others. There's a good chance they end up solving ten to twelve, but not all twenty-four. Do we often see dramatic progress after solving just two or three? Yes, often we do.

What's the blueprint for our Low Acuity students? These students, as you'll recall, have fewer unsolved problems and their behaviors are at a level of severity that can be handled in the general ed classroom. Clearly Tier 1, if you're keeping track. Here's the sequence of events for these students:

1. Identify unsolved problems.
2. If, in keeping with Tier 1, you first want to make sure that the student is clear about what's being expected, that's great; however, there's only a very a slim chance doing so will obviate the need for Plan B.
3. Do Plan B, using the Early Problems Worksheet (EPW) to formally keep track.

Should identifying what's making it hard for a student to meet an expectation through Plan B be standard practice at Tier 1? No question. The information gathered through Plan B *informs* and *facilitates* differentiation. The student's voice is indispensable. And, as you've read, the information gathered from students frequently differs from what adults had assumed or hypothesized about what was making it hard for a student to meet an expectation.

Here are two potential scenarios for what that could look like. In the first scenario, a fourth-grade teacher learns that what she *thought* was getting in the way of a student meeting an expectation is *not* what is getting in the way.

Teacher (Empathy step): *Juanita, I've noticed you've been having difficulty getting started on the sentences after reading the paragraphs in ELA. What's up?*

Juanita: *It's too noisy in ELA. Everyone's talking to each other.*

Teacher: *Yes, it is kind of noisy in ELA, since we do the sentences with a partner and everyone's talking to each other.* (The teacher had theorized that Juanita didn't like her partner and/or was having difficulty with some aspect of writing the sentences, so she was surprised by this piece of information. She had previously switched Juanita's partners several times and had considered that Juanita might benefit from some supports around writing sentences.) *So, it's not because of who your partner is?*

Juanita: *No, I don't really care who my partner is, as long as I don't have to work with Matt.*

Teacher: *Yes, I know that Matt and you sometimes don't work very well together. And it's not because writing the sentences is hard for you?*

Juanita: *No, I don't have any trouble writing the sentences.*

Teacher: *So, it's too noisy in ELA. That's good for me to know. Is there anything else making it hard for you to get started on the sentences after reading the paragraphs in ELA?*

Juanita: *Well, sometimes I don't have a pencil to write with.*

Teacher: *Ah, yes, sometimes you do ask me if I have a pencil you can use. You know, you don't have to ask me for a pencil. You can just go to the cabinet and get one if you don't have one.*

Juanita: *Oh, OK.*

Teacher: *So, the reasons you're having difficulty getting started on writing the sentences after reading the paragraphs in ELA is because it's too noisy and sometimes because you don't have a pencil. Is there anything else?*

Juanita: *I can't think of anything else.*

Teacher (Define Adult Concerns step): *OK, my concern is that I really want to make sure you get practice at writing about what you read, and if you aren't writing the sentences, you won't be getting the practice and I won't be able to tell if you're getting good at that. Do you understand what I mean?*
Juanita: *Yes.*
Teacher (Invitation step): *So, I wonder if there's a way for us to do something about the noise bothering you in ELA and also make sure that you get practice at writing so I can tell if you're getting good at that. Do you have any ideas?*
Juanita: *Last year I used those headphones, so the noise didn't bother me. But I can't use headphones if I'm working with a partner. Do I have to work with a partner?*
Teacher: *Well, I would like you to work with a partner. But it's more important to me that you get practice at writing the sentences. I wonder if there are any other solutions so you could still work with a partner?*
Juanita: *Maybe me and my partner could work out in the hall. Then the noise wouldn't bother me and I could still work with a partner.*
Teacher: *Are you OK with that? I don't want you to work out in the hall if that's not OK with you.*
Juanita: *I like working out in the hall . . . it's nice and quiet most of the time.*

In this next scenario, things turn in a different direction with a different student (but the same unsolved problem), again based on the information provided by the student:

Teacher: *I've noticed you've been having difficulty getting started on the sentences after reading the paragraphs in ELA. What's up?*
Dexter: *I don't understand the paragraphs, so I can't write the sentences.*

Teacher: *You don't understand the paragraphs. I didn't know that. Can you tell me more about that?*

Dexter: *The words are too hard for me. And then you want me to write paragraphs about something I couldn't read in the first place.*

Teacher: *This is very good for me to know. Is it all the words or just some?*

Dexter: *Not all.*

Teacher: *Can you show me? How about we look at one of the paragraphs you've had to read, and you can tell me which words are hard for you?*

(The teacher and student examine a paragraph and Dexter points out the words he couldn't read.)

Teacher (moving into the Define Adult Concerns step): *This is very helpful, Dexter: Thank you for showing me. My concern is that I really want to make sure you get practice at writing about what you read, and if you aren't writing the sentences, you won't be getting the practice and I won't be able to tell if you're getting good at that. Do you understand what I mean?*

Dexter: *Yes. But how can I write about it if I can't read it?*

Teacher (Invitation step): *Exactly. So, I wonder if there's something we can do about you having difficulty reading some of the words and also make sure that you're getting practice at writing the sentences. Do you have any ideas?*

Dexter: *I don't want to ask my partner to explain the words I can't read. It's embarrassing. Could you give me paragraphs that I would be able to read?*

Teacher: *Dexter, I like that idea very much. How about we pull out some different paragraphs so you can let me know which ones you can read and which ones you can't? Of course, we'll also want to find a way for you to know what to do when there's a word you can't read or don't understand. But we can talk about that another time.*

Again, if the classroom teacher wanted to formalize recordkeeping on these conversations, they could complete the Early Problems Worksheet (EPW).

You might be thinking that the above dialogues went rather seamlessly (again). No doubt there are some students who don't respond after you say, "What's up?" Some who say, "I don't know." Others who say, "I don't have a problem with that," or "I don't care." There are some who say, "I don't want to talk about it right now." Others who become defensive and say, "I don't have to talk to you" (or worse). Still others who are nonspeaking and can't participate in the conversation through the spoken word. And still others who don't have any ideas for solutions. We'll cover those possibilities in chapter 7. But the steps of Plan B are the same with all students.

The more Plan B we do with Low Acuity students, the less likely they are to become High Acuity students.

Even Earlier

As you've read, the ASUP and Plan B are upstream. Way upstream. But the above guidelines kick in once a student is already having difficulty meeting expectations. Are there practices that could kick in well before that happens? Yes, indeed.

Differentiated Instruction: For the unfamiliar, differentiated instruction refers to the practice of tailoring instruction to meet the diverse needs, learning styles, readiness levels, and interests of individual students within a classroom. Instead of using a one-size-fits-all method, teachers vary the content (what students learn), process (how students learn), product (how students show what they know), or learning environment so that all students have access to meaningful learning. Differentiated instruction is grounded in the belief that students learn best when teachers accommodate differences rather than trying to eliminate them. If teachers aren't skilled in differentiating instruction, training needs to be provided as early as possible, even before the school year begins. If teachers don't have permission to differentiate—perhaps because they're under pressure to get everyone over the same bar by the end of the school year, or because the instructional schedule is so regimented, or because they're worried about being out of compliance with a student's IEP—we need to address those issues at a systemic level.

Mentality and Mission: Establishing the mentality and mission of a building is earlier still. Why are we here? What do we do in our building? How do we do it? If we don't have an established mentality and mission, we can't possibly be on the same page and we can't possibly be clear about our expectations for staff or students. Here are some suggestions to guide thinking about mentality and mission and aid in the creation of mission statements. As you'd imagine, we've covered some of these themes already.

- The overriding philosophy about students is *Kids do well if they can.* This is the belief that if a student could do well, they would do well, and that if they aren't doing well, something must be getting in the way. What's getting in the way? Skills (if they're responding poorly to problems and frustrations) and unsolved problems. What do we do if a student isn't doing well on a particular task? Solve the problem, collaboratively and proactively. By the way, *Kids do well if they can* represents a dramatic departure from the more traditional mentality of *Kids do well if they want to.* The latter simply causes us to think the student doesn't want to do well, default to motivational explanations, and commence with the process of incentivizing the student to do well. This is worth repeating: rewards and punishments are not problem-solving strategies.

- When it comes to expectations, *every student is their own reference point.* So, while we have expectations for all students, they are somewhat *different for everyone.*
- When a student is struggling to meet an expectation, *we focus on the expectation they're struggling to meet* (the unsolved problem), rather than the concerning behaviors that are being caused by the unsolved problem.
- If we wait for the behavior to occur to signal that a student is having difficulty meeting an expectation, we're going to be late every time.
- If we don't identify unsolved problems proactively, we won't be able to solve them proactively.
- Relationships with students are paramount and a primary focal point. But we recognize that, as important as they are, relationships alone do not solve any problems. So, relationship-building, while critical, isn't sufficient. And solving problems collaboratively is going to build those relationships for us.

Here's a sample mission statement:

We strive to provide whatever it takes to ensure that students are successful academically, socially, and emotionally and reach their highest potential. Our school is student-centered, safe, and nurturing, and we employ strategies that are non-punitive, non-exclusionary, and relationship- and skill-enhancing. We meet students where they're at, value individual differences, and strive to collaboratively solve the problems that are interfering with their success.

Just an example. It's your school. But you get the idea.

Before the School Year Begins: Problems that arise in the first weeks of school aren't typically new or surprising. The long arc of a student's trajectory begins way before the student walks into a new classroom on Day One. So, we're already behind the late eight ball if this year's teachers haven't received the right information from last year's teachers about a given student. Often, even when information is passed along, it's about a student's *behavior* and *diagnoses* rather than about their skills and unsolved problems. That is not the most critical or actionable information. This year's teachers also need to know what worked and what didn't in previous years. If your school doesn't have a formal mechanism in place so that last year's teacher(s) can pass information along to this year's teacher(s), you're setting people up to be late.

Inviting students to visit their new teachers or school before the year begins is also an excellent practice. Having kids write down what they want their new teachers to know about them is an excellent practice too. Meeting with parents before the year begins, especially the parents of students who struggled the year before, to initiate communication, get relationships established, and obtain their thoughts about what works and what doesn't with their child is far preferable to waiting until things head south.

Q & A

Question: I love your "pool" of services concept. Do you have anything more to say about that?

Answer: As a matter of fact, yes! That pool of supports and services is also best conceived as a *continuum of care*. That continuum should be centered on long-term growth rather than immediate remediation. The goal is to adapt to students' evolving needs, more akin to lifelong wellness programs rather than short-term medical treatment. With the exception of medication miracles, students do not typically "recover" from their difficulties in the way that patients with acute medical issues recover from an illness; instead, they receive ongoing, responsive instruction that helps them overcome those difficulties progressively and incrementally. This broader view shifts the focus from "fixing" students to supporting them at every stage of their development.

Question: I'm a general education classroom teacher, and some of what you've described in this chapter is outside of my control. Are my special education director and superintendent going to be reading this book?
Answer: We certainly hope your special education director and superintendent read this book. (Several have provided feedback prior to publication, so we're not just tilting at windmills here.) And it's important to put these ideas out there even if not everyone reading this book can impact policies and procedures directly. We have to get the conversation going.

Question: My school has invested heavily in PBIS and tiered interventions. Are you saying we should abandon that?
Answer: Not necessarily. The CPS model can be integrated into existing tiered structures, but we do encourage you to look closely at whether your current system is reactive or proactive and focused on concerning behavior or unsolved problems. The tiers shouldn't drive the work; the students' needs should. We just think school staff should spend more time talking about what a student actually needs—and forming those conclusions based on information they gathered from the student—than talking about tiers.

Question: So, saying that a student is at Tier 1 really isn't saying much?
Answer: Well, it's saying something about *who's doing what* but it isn't saying anything about what a student needs.

Question: On the "pool" of services concept, I need to get into the weeds here. Our state regulations say that a student's need for special education and related services is determined by whether, *because of a disability,* the student child can neither progress effectively in a regular education program nor receive reasonable benefit from such a program despite other services available to the child. We establish that by determining whether there is a distinctly measurable and persistent *gap* in the child's educational or functional performance that cannot be addressed through services or accommodations available through the general education program. What are your thoughts about those structures?
Answer: We understand that's the traditional way of defining and doing things, and, as we noted, it's very adult-driven. So many decisions are made *for* kids without information *from* kids. What we're urging educators to think about is the value added by gathering information from kids before adults kick into high gear, and the fact that such information can change the game completely. We're also urging moving away from gaps and eligibility and toward focusing on problems and solving them. Then we're in a much better position to determine whether the student needs anything from the deep end of the pool.

Question: I'm a bit speechless. These structures—tiers, special education—that we've been relying on forever . . . they don't help us be proactive, and they don't help us triage either.
Answer: Sometimes structures that made sense at one time don't make as much sense over time. The trick is to adapt when things aren't working as well as they could.

Question: And the new structures would not only be better for the kids but also for us educators.
Answer: That's right.

Question: It pains me to think of all the kids who might have been better served if we'd been seeking information from them rather than plugging them into services they might not have needed.
Answer: It was painful for the kids too.

Question: It sounds like you're questioning the wisdom of the Individual with Disabilities Education Act (IDEA). Are you?
Answer: We're not questioning the importance of the funding provided by IDEA and the number of students it has helped. We're questioning the onerousness and inefficiency of the processes that have made that help harder for students to access. As we've described, we think those processes need to be revamped.

Question: Why didn't they teach me about Plan B when I was trained as a teacher?
Answer: It would have been good if they had.

Question: You still haven't talked about when I'm going to find the time to do this.
Answer: We will.

Closer Look: Pushing Upstream

In his excellent book *Upstream: The Quest to Solve Problems Before They Happen*, author Dan Heath makes some cogent points about the benefits of being proactive and why that can be so hard to do. "When you spend years responding to problems, you can sometimes overlook the fact that you could be preventing them." He speaks to what can make it hard to change things. "So often in life, we get stuck in a cycle of response. We put out fires. We deal with emergencies. We handle one problem after another, but we never get around to fixing the systems that caused the problems. How many problems in our lives and society are we tolerating simply because we've forgotten that we can fix them?"

The first step, of course, is to recognize that there is a problem. Heath writes, "You can't solve a problem that you can't see, or one that you perceive as a regrettable but inevitable condition of life."

It's also important to recognize the critical importance of being early. Heath writes, "We can—and we should—stop dealing with the symptoms of problems, again and again, and start fixing them. We can intervene at many points along an almost limitless timeline. In other words, you don't head upstream, as in a specific destination. You head upstream as in a direction. To go upstream is a declaration of agency: I don't have to be at the mercy of these forces. I can shape my world."

The trick is to energize around the idea that things could be better and to get started. "Systems change starts with a spark of courage. A group of people unite around a common cause, and they demand change. But a spark can't last forever. The endgame is to eliminate the need for courage, to render it unnecessary, because it has forced change within the system. Success comes when the right things happen by default . . . success comes when the odds have shifted."

. . . .

"Swim upstream. Go the other way. Ignore the conventional wisdom."

—Sam Walton

7

Questions About Plan B

The best way to get a feel for what Plan B looks like, along with its technicalities and nuances, is to see it in action and practice it. So, we really think it's best for you to watch some videos of Plan B on the Lives in the Balance website before getting caught up in the weeds. That said, we've devoted this chapter to answering some of the most common questions about Plan B.

Question: Some of my students are very compromised in the language processing and communication realm. Is it realistic that I can solve problems collaboratively with them?
Answer: In a word, yes. As you'd imagine, in a model that relies so heavily on gathering information from kids, we've developed a variety of strategies for moving things along when kids are having difficulty participating in Plan B. We've often distinguished between kids who can talk but aren't and those who aren't talking because they can't. Though our approach to those two populations is conceptually the same, the strategies tend to be different.

In kids who can talk but aren't, often the reason they aren't talking—you read about this earlier—is because we've been trying to talk with them about their concerning behavior, which only causes them to think they're in trouble, become defensive, and stop talking. You'll have far greater success if you're gathering information from them about expectations they've been having difficulty meeting, often for a very long time. Some of the kids who can talk but aren't may not trust you or the process yet; fortunately, engaging kids in Plan B is very trust-engendering (though not instantaneously), so hang in there. Others haven't thought about their concerns for a very long time, so accustomed have they become to having their concerns dismissed or disregarded. Still others have lost faith in us adults, after many years of having problems go unsolved. Others just need time to think. You can read about the many strategies we apply to this population in an earlier book—*Lost at School*—but ultimately, if a kid isn't able to provide information in the Empathy step, one of our go-to's is to find a way for the kid to signal—often by holding up fingers—their agreement with guesses we're making about what's making it hard for them to meet an expectation.

And the kids who aren't talking because they can't? Also a very heterogeneous population. First, we should acknowledge that, thanks to assistive technology, there's never been a better time in human evolution to help those kids communicate. But some nonspeaking kids are communicating in ways that caregivers can't yet comprehend and aren't yet able to utilize assistive technologies. With those kids, we have a singular goal: find *some way* (grunts, gestures, hand signals) for them to formally communicate about *something* (that something is wrong, pain, or the need for sensory input). We need to get the ball rolling in some manner; once we have a foothold, we can branch out from there. There are more details about this population as well in *Lost at School.*

Question: Does Plan B hold kids accountable for their actions?

Answer: Yes, and a whole lot more effectively than consequences do. When you're imposing consequences for a student's concerning behavior, the student is the passive recipient of your actions. No thinking. No engagement. No accountability. When you're solving problems using

Plan B, the student is fully engaged in the process of solving the problems that are causing their concerning behavior. That's accountability.

Question: Don't you think there are some behaviors that are so egregious that we have to use consequences? Even if it's just to placate the parents of other kids who were victimized by those behaviors?
Answer: As you know, we don't rank frustration responses by their severity. And we don't think you should do something you think isn't going to work to placate anyone. The parents of kids who are victimized want you to do something to make sure their kid isn't victimized again far more than they want to be placated. But if you feel that you have no choice—perhaps because you're mandated to use consequences by the policies and procedures of your school system—then consequences you shall use. Just make sure you're also doing what you're reading in this book, because you still have to do something that will actually be effective.

Question: So you don't think kids are doing more poorly these days because we've gone soft?
Answer: No, we do not. And there's nothing soft about what you're reading in this book. The kids who aren't doing OK have often been on the receiving end of more adult-imposed consequences than most of us will experience in this lifetime. If that's the definition of hard, it hasn't worked.

Question: Are you saying that adults are no longer on the hook for teaching skills to kids?
Answer: No way. Adults effectively teach kids lots of skills: math, reading, writing, spelling, how to enter a group, how to start a conversation, sharing, taking turns . . . we could go on forever. We just have doubts about whether the skills of flexibility/adaptability, frustration tolerance, problem-solving, and emotion regulation are best taught through direct

instruction or through a curriculum. We think those skills are best enhanced through a process and through experience . . . the process and experience of solving problems collaboratively and proactively. Plan B doesn't just solve problems . . . it models and gives kids practice at those skills. The problems are going to get solved way faster than the skills are going to get enhanced. So you won't have to wait until the skills improve before you see dramatic improvements in behavior. Again, you're improving behavior by solving the problems that are causing them. The skill enhancement is the icing on the cake.

Question: What if the kid says "I don't care" in response to "What's up?" in the Empathy step. How can we solve a problem if the kid doesn't care about it?
Answer: The kid doesn't have to care about the problem; it's your expectation, so you're the one who cares about it. So "I don't care" is actually just the beginning of the kid's concern or perspective. Start drilling, starting with reflective listening.

Question: What if the kid says "I don't want to talk about it right now" in response to "What's up?" in the Empathy step?
Answer: First, give them permission not to talk about it right now. Lots of kids start talking the minute you give them permission not to. If that doesn't get you there, there's probably a good reason they don't want to talk about it right now. Maybe they'll talk about that first.

Question: What if the kid says "I'm not talking to you" or worse in response to "What's up?" in the Empathy step?
Answer: Stay honest with the kid. Say, "You don't have to talk to me right now." And if they say "You're not my boss," say "I'm not your boss." And if they say "You can't make me talk," say "I can't make you talk." Some

kids are so disarmed by the honesty that they start talking. You might also want to reassure the kids that they're not in trouble (because they're not), you're not mad at them (because you're not), you're not going to impose a solution (because you're not), and all you're trying to do is understand (because you are).

Question: Is it OK to start thinking about solutions in the Empathy step?
Answer: Technically, you can't think about solutions in the Empathy step because you haven't done the Define Adult Concerns step yet and the solution is supposed to address the concerns of both parties. Plus, it would be quite distracting to be thinking of solutions in the Empathy step; what you should be thinking about is whether you understand what the kid said and whether you need to drill further.

Question: What if I disagree with what the kid is saying in the Empathy step?
Answer: The kid is entitled to their point of view. Their concerns are as legitimate as yours.

Question: What if I think the kid is lying in the Empathy step?
Answer: We don't worry about lying in the Empathy step, since all you're trying to do is ascertain what's making it hard for the kid to meet a particular expectation. The demand for lying comes when you're doing Plan A, because the kid thinks they're in trouble and might anticipate the lowering of the boom.

Question: Aren't adult concerns more important than the kid's concerns?
Answer: The concerns of both parties are of exactly equal legitimacy. And they both need to be addressed for the problem to be solved. Your goal is

to demonstrate to the kid that you're as invested in getting their concerns addressed as you are in getting your own concerns addressed.

Question: What if a solution doesn't work or stops working?
Answer: That usually happens for one or more of three possible reasons. Possibility number one is that the solution wasn't as realistic as you thought it was. That's a good reason to go back to Plan B to collaborate on a solution that is more realistic. Possibility number two is that the solution wasn't as mutually satisfactory as you thought it was. That too is a good reason to go back to Plan B to collaborate on a solution that is mutually satisfactory. Possibility number three is that there are other concerns that need to be addressed that weren't addressed by the first solution. Back to Plan B to figure that out and address those concerns.

Question: Isn't Plan B just common sense?
Answer: We hear that a lot. Regrettably, it's uncommon common sense.

• • • • • • •

"Tell me and I forget. Teach me and I remember. Involve me and I learn."
—Benjamin Franklin

"When we give children advice or instant solutions, we deprive them of the experience that comes from wrestling with their own problems."
—Adele Faber

8

....

Your Lane

In chapter 1 we described the various mental health challenges facing today's kids, with sky-high rates of depression, anxiety, concerning behavior, suicidality, and chronic school absenteeism topping the list. And we established that caregivers are struggling even more than the kids. Can educators do anything about those mental health and family challenges?

Possibly. While there will be times when you'll want to seek out, or connect the student with, someone who has greater expertise with a particular mental health disorder or issue (e.g., the school psychologist, an outside mental health practitioner), just because a student's difficulties involve "mental health" or "family" rather than "education" doesn't mean you have to abandon ship. If a student is confiding in you and trusting you with important information, they chose *you* for a good reason. You must be doing something right. While it's OK to let the student know you may not be able to take them all the way to a solution and that they may need more expertise than you can offer, keep gathering information and listening.

As you read in chapter 1, there's a lot of overlap between education and mental health. Mental health practitioners listen, as do educators. Mental health practitioners try to understand what's making things hard for people, as do educators. And mental health practitioners help people solve the problems that are affecting their lives; educators do that too. So it's not like you're completely a fish out of water (though you may be out of your comfort zone on some issues).

Are there going to be kids who are harder to engage in the problem-solving process than others? Definitely. Some kids are going to be very skeptical of the process—skeptical of adults in general—given that they may have a long history of having their concerns dismissed or disregarded and/or may have had many experiences with adults who made things worse. Plan B should convince them that you're not talking with them about their concerning behavior (a showstopper), that you're not about to lower the boom (another showstopper), that you're not angry (still another), and that you're trustworthy and deeply devoted to understanding and helping them with their struggles (the door just cracked open). Some kids lose style points on how they deliver the information, perhaps because their anger or frustration has been bottled up for many years. The information you obtain in the Empathy step of Plan B is more important than how it's delivered.

And there are going to be some unsolved problems that you might need the parents to help you solve, especially the ones on which there is overlap between home and school. But not that many. Here are the top five:

- Difficulty coming to school
- Difficulty coming to school on time
- Difficulty coming to school well-clothed, well-fed, and well-slept
- Difficulty completing certain homework assignments
- Difficulty separating from parents to come into the building in the morning

On those, it would be ideal if you can get parental involvement. But if you can't, you're still in business. You can still gather information from students about what's making it hard for them to come to school; hard for them to get to school on time; come to school well-clothed, well-fed, and well slept; complete specific homework assignments; and separate from their parent(s) to come into the building. The information you obtain will let you know whether you really need help from the home folks to come to a solution. And if the home folks won't participate in the process, you may have to come up with solutions that don't involve them. As you shall soon read.

Below you'll be reading some examples of how mental health and family issues can overlap with some commonplace school-related unsolved problems. We'll be helping you think about the points at which the student might need more help than you can provide. And we'll be providing tips on some of the nuances of Plan B.

....

This first one is rather brief, depicting only the beginning of an Empathy step.

Student: *Travis, fifth grader*
Diagnoses: *Panic disorder; separation anxiety*
Concerning Behavior: *Has panic attacks when being dropped off at school, including kicking and screaming when adults try to force him to enter the building.*
Hypothesis: *Though he's always been a little separation anxious, the parents' divorce has made Travis feel less secure being away from them; also, anxiety runs in the family.*
What Plan A Could Look Like: *Reward Travis for coming into the building with no problem; ultimately, physically escort him into the building if coaxing him doesn't work (he's always OK once he stops kicking and screaming). Encourage the parents to talk to the pediatrician*

so that anti-anxiety medication can be prescribed and to obtain a referral to a mental health clinician so Travis can talk about the divorce.

Wording of Unsolved Problem: *Difficulty coming into the building when dad drops you off in the morning.*

Adult: I've noticed you have difficulty coming into the building when your dad drops you off in the morning. What's up? *And here we go. First, notice that you're not trying to get the conversation started by asking Travis about his concerning behavior (panic attacks, kicking, and screaming). You're sticking with the unsolved problem: the expectation Travis is having difficulty meeting. That's your entry point. Let's see how the conversation progresses (or doesn't) from there.*

Travis: I don't know. *(Not a great start, but also not uncommon. Let's give Travis time to think.)*

Adult, reflective listening: You don't know. Well, think about it. We're not in a rush. I know that's been hard for you for a while.

Travis: I don't really want to do this right now. *(Some reluctance from Travis, but not a deal-breaker.)*

Adult, reflective listening, with a clarifying statement: You don't want to do this right now. Help me understand that better.

Travis: You didn't tell me that's what you wanted to talk with me about. *(It's always good to give kids advance notice of what you want to talk with them about; otherwise, you're surprising them with the topic even if you're doing Plan B proactively.)*

Adult, reflective listening: You are right about that, Travis. I did not tell you what I wanted to talk with you about. I guess I messed that up.

Travis: Yeah, so, I don't know if I want to talk about that right now.

Adult: We don't have to talk about that right now. We can do it another time. Unless you feel like you can help me understand that better even though I didn't give you advance notice.

Travis: Um . . . it's just that I don't really like coming to school.

Adult, reflective listening with a clarifying question: Ah, you don't really like coming to school. Thank you for telling me that. Can you tell me more? *(Notice, the adult isn't feeling any pressure to divine what Travis means when he says he doesn't like coming to school. Asking is better.)*

Travis: I'm like, one of the dumbest kids in the class. And the only things people work on with me are the things I'm not good at.

Adult, asking a W question (Drilling Strategy #2): I think I know what you mean. But can we be a little more specific? What are the things you feel you're not good at?

This would obviously be a much longer Empathy step, covering all the parts of the school day the student doesn't feel confident about. But note that simple reflective listening—which was the primary drilling strategy the adult used—was effective at helping the student feel heard, clarify their concerns, feel understood, feel like the adult cared and was truly interested in understanding, and kept them talking. And though the conversation could have gone in a bunch of different directions, some of which *could* have suggested that parental involvement was necessary or that it *might* be useful to consult with someone with expertise in panic attacks, there's also some chance that solving the different problems Travis is having at school—along with the relationship-building that occurs in the course of doing Plan B—will help him come into the building more readily. In other words, the panic disorder and separation anxiety may resolve once the problem is solved. Travis hasn't said anything about his parents' divorce or feeling insecure about being away from them. So, it's not clear that the parents or outside experts are needed to help solve this one.

Let's try another one.

. . . .

This next Empathy step does end up focusing on a student's family.

Student: *Sheila, seventh grader*
Diagnoses: *Depression? Social anxiety?*
Concerning Behavior: *No interaction with peers during recess and lunch; stands or sits off by herself; when permitted, prefers to stay in the classroom while the other kids are at recess and lunch.*
Hypothesis: *She's shy and lacking important social skills and needs a referral to the school counselor so she can participate in a social skills group.*
What Plan A Could Look Like: *Place her in a social skills group with the school counselor.*
Wording of Unsolved Problem: *Difficulty hanging out with peers during recess.*
Adult: I've noticed you have difficulty hanging out with the other kids during recess. What's up?
Sheila: *(Silence. Also not a promising start, but not uncommon and not catastrophic.)*
Adult, after thirty seconds: Take your time. We're not in a rush.
Sheila: *(Silence.)*
Adult, after another thirty seconds: Do you know what you want to say but you're not sure how to say it or are you not sure what to say? *(Sometimes a good question to ask to get your bearings on what's making it hard for a kid to talk.)*
Sheila: I . . . know what I want to say. But I don't *want* to say it.
Adult, reflective listening with a clarifying question: Ah, you know what you want to say but you don't want to say it. Can you tell me more about that?
Sheila: If I tell you and then you say something to the other kids, it'll be worse.

Adult, reflective listening: Ah, so you're concerned that if you say what you want to say and I say something about it to the other kids, things could be worse than they are now.

Sheila: *(Nodding.)*

Adult: And what if I promised that what you tell me is just between me and you?

Sheila: I would tell you.

Adult: Unless you tell me something that makes me think you could be unsafe, I promise that what you tell me is just between me and you.

Sheila: The other kids are kinda mean to me. So I kinda stay away from them.

Adult: Thank you for telling me that. How are the other kids mean to you?

Sheila: *(Silence.)*

Adult, after thirty seconds: Can you tell me how the other kids are mean to you? Because I haven't seen that. *(Oops . . . let's not say that last part . . . Sheila is entitled to her reality whether you've seen it or not . . . and we don't want to express skepticism about Sheila's concerns, or she may stop talking entirely. Let's pretend the last sentence didn't happen.)*

Sheila: They know I live in my mom's boyfriend's trailer.

Adult, reflective listening: They know you live in your mom's boyfriend's trailer.

Sheila: And they know my mom is in jail right now. And so . . . it's just me and her boyfriend in the trailer.

Adult, reflective listening: They know your mom is in jail and it's just you and her boyfriend living in the trailer. *(If the adult is now starting to think about being a mandated reporter or having someone else with more expertise get involved, that's fine. But let's drill further to see if either option is necessary.)*

Sheila: And it's OK . . . I don't mind being with my mom's boyfriend. He's nice and everything. But kids say stuff.

Adult: *(Possibly wishing someone else was leading this conversation, but glad the student is talking to them, and still using reflective listening, followed by a W question.)* You don't mind being with your mother's boyfriend because he's nicer than your mom, but people say stuff. What kind of things do people say?

Sheila: *(Silence.)*

Adult, after thirty seconds: Can you tell me what people say?

Sheila: They say he's my boyfriend. They say . . . we're having sex.

Adult, reflective listening: They say he's your boyfriend. And that you're having sex with him.

Sheila: This is embarrassing.

Adult: I bet. But I'm glad we're talking about it. Do you feel safe around your mom's boyfriend? *(Important mandated reporter question.)*

Sheila: Yeah. I mean, he's been her boyfriend since I was, like, three. He's more like a father.

Adult: So, what the kids are saying is untrue.

Sheila: Of course!

Adult: Do you want to tell me who's saying those things?

Sheila: No.

Adult: Do you want to tell me about your mom being in jail? I didn't know about that.

Sheila: She got a DUI.

Adult: Got it. How long will she be in jail?

Sheila: We don't know yet.

Adult: Do the kids say mean things about that too?

Sheila: *(Nodding, tearing up.)*

Adult, after thirty seconds: You still OK talking about this?

Sheila: *(Nodding.)*

Adult, summarizing and asking for more: So, let me summarize what you've told me so far. One of the reasons you're not hanging out with other kids at recess is because they're saying unkind things about you living in a trailer with your mom's boyfriend. And they're also saying unkind things about your mom being in jail. Is there anything else making it hard for you to hang out with the other kids at recess?

Sheila: No, it just feels like everybody's snickering about those things, so I don't feel comfortable hanging out with anybody. I mean, I could fight the people who are saying mean things, I guess, but then I'd get in trouble.

Nice drilling. Nice caring. The Empathy step might be done, though we'd recommend summarizing and asking for more one more time before moving on to the Define Adult Concerns step and the Invitation step. Based on the information gathered, do we need to make a referral to a social service agency? Not yet. A referral to a mental health professional? Not yet. Do we need to see if the boyfriend will come in for a meeting? Not yet. What's the solution? Well, we haven't done the Define Adult Concerns step yet, so we're not ready for the Invitation step yet. And, as always, we'd want Sheila to participate in the formulation of a solution. (We provide an example of all three steps of Plan B later in the chapter, and, of course, there's always those videos you can watch.) But let's move on to another.

....

Student: *Carson, tenth grader in an alternative school*

Diagnoses: *ADHD, conduct disorder?*

Concerning Behavior: *Skipping school*

Hypothesis: *His mother is overwhelmed by work and her four other children. He may be in a gang.*

What Plan A Could Look Like: *Refer the family to social services.*

Wording of Unsolved Problem: *Difficulty coming to school.*

Adult: Carson, good to see you today!

Carson: Uh-huh.

Adult: We're always happy when you're here.

Carson: Why?

Adult: We like having you here. You're an important member of our community.

Carson: Uh-huh.

Adult: But it's hard for you to get here, yes?

Carson: Uh-huh.

Adult: What's making it hard for you to get here? *(We're not religious about the wording of the Introduction to the Empathy step, so this minor deviation isn't catastrophic.)*

Carson: It's just hard.

Adult: Can you tell me what's hard about it?

Carson: Number one, my mom isn't always home from work on time, so I have to watch my brothers and sisters.

Adult, reflective listening: Ah, your mom isn't always home from work on time and you have to watch your brothers and sisters.

Carson: Well, my grandmother is supposed to come over when my mom is running late, but sometimes she doesn't.

Adult, summarizing and asking for more: Got it. So one of the reasons you're having difficulty getting to school is because your mom sometimes doesn't get home from work on time and you have to watch your brothers and sisters. And your grandmother isn't always able to watch them.

Carson: Yep.

Adult: Are there any other reasons you're having difficulty getting to school?

Carson: Well, since I miss so much, I'm always behind. So, like, what's the point in showing up?

Adult, reflective listening: Ah, since you miss so much school you're always behind and it feels like there's no point in showing up.

Carson: Yep. So I don't think there's much you can do about these things.

Adult: Maybe not. We'll see. But I'm glad you're helping me understand.

Carson: If you're thinking of reporting us to social services, it's already happened a bunch of times.

Adult: I wasn't thinking of doing that. But let's think about what you've told me already. You're having difficulty getting here because your mom doesn't always get home from work in time for you to get to school. And your grandma can't always get there to watch your brothers and sisters. And since you miss a lot and you're always behind you don't see much point in showing up. Do I have it right?

Carson: Yep.

Adult: Anything else making it hard for you to come to school?

Carson: Well, I have to take, like, three different trains and buses to get here. Because I have to stay away from certain neighborhoods. Because of gangs.

Adult: OK. So you also have to take several trains and buses to get here because of gangs. Are you in a gang?

Carson: No. But it's still not safe to go through those neighborhoods.

Adult, tabling: You're really doing a great job of helping me understand. So if your mom wasn't getting home from work late, and if your grandma could always watch your brothers and sisters, and if you didn't mind being behind on things, and if you didn't have to take several forms of transportation, would there be anything else making it hard for you to get to school? (That's a drilling strategy called *tabling.*)

Carson: Well, I mean, even with all that stuff going on . . . I guess I could get here . . . I just don't like showing up late and having everyone look at me.

Adult: Ah, got it. So you don't like having everyone looking at you when you show up late.

Carson: It's kind of embarrassing.

Adult: Help me understand that better.

Carson: I just don't like having everyone looking at me. It makes me uncomfortable. And kids give me a hard time about it sometimes. I just don't feel like dealing with that.

Adult: Got it. So . . . out of all those things you told me . . . your mom doesn't always get home from work on time, your grandma can't always watch your brothers and sisters, you have to take several forms of transportation to get here, you're behind already and don't see the point in showing up, and you're embarrassed about being late and the kids give you a hard time about it . . . which is most important? Which is getting in the way the most? *(Carson has a lot of concerns related to this unsolved problem, which is fairly typical, but you won't be able to address all of them with the same solution; so before moving on from the Empathy step, you'll want to ask the student which of the concerns is most important or getting in the way the most. That's the one you'll try to address in this Plan B; you may need separate Plan Bs for the others.)*

Carson: Being behind and not seeing the point in showing up. I mean, I guess I can deal with the other stuff.

Adult: How about we work on that one and then go back to the others if we need to?

There's still some more sorting out to do—for example, Carson might be further behind in some classes than others—but it's good that he's talking, feeling heard, and confiding, and that we're listening, trying to understand, caring, and offering hope. The Define Adult Concerns step and Invitation step would come after that. Can you do anything about his mother coming home late from work, his grandmother sometimes being unable to watch his siblings, or the gangs he must avoid? Unlikely. But you don't have to solve everything to make progress. And you don't want to let the concerns you can't address keep you from addressing the ones you can.

One more?

....

Student: *Aroldis, kindergartener*
Diagnoses: *ADHD (for which he is medicated), autism spectrum disorder*
Concerning Behavior: *Hitting kids when they want him to play with them*
Hypothesis: *It's the impulsiveness (of the ADHD) and the difficulty appreciating how his behavior is affecting others (of the autism) causing the hitting.*
What Plan A Could Look Like: *Escort him to the Calming Corner after he hits kids; teach and reteach replacement behaviors for hitting; reward him when he doesn't hit for the day. Talk to the parents to mention to the pediatrician that the dose of the medicine might need to be increased. Referral to the school counselor so Aroldis can participate in some social skills exercises.*
Wording of Unsolved Problem: *Difficulty keeping body safe during choice time.*
Adult: I've noticed you have difficulty keeping your body safe during choice time. What's up?
Aroldis: That's a nice picture over there.
Adult, turning to look at the picture on the wall: Yes, it is. You mean the one with the canoe?

Aroldis: Uh-huh.

Adult, observing whether Aroldis is zoned back in: So, what do you think? Can you tell me any reasons it's been hard to keep your body safe during choice time?

Aroldis: Are we going out for recess today?

Adult: I can't think of any reason why we wouldn't. The weather's good. So I'm betting we go out for recess today. Is there something you really want to do at recess today?

Aroldis: I just like running around.

Adult: Ah, yes, I've seen you run around a lot during recess.

Aroldis: And, also, Ali and I have a club.

Adult: A club! Fun!

Aroldis: Uh-huh. So that's why I was hoping we go out for recess today.

Adult: I get it. So, do you remember what I asked you about in the beginning?

Aroldis: Why I don't use a safe body during choice time?

Adult: Yes! What can you tell me about that?

Aroldis: Everyone's bugging me to play with them.

Adult, reflective listening, followed by a clarifying statement: Everyone's bugging you to play with them. Tell me more.

Aroldis: Everyone wants me to play with them and I can't play with everyone but they keep bugging me and so I have to hit them to get them to stop.

Adult, summarizing and asking for more: Ah, I think I'm starting to understand. So, during choice time, everyone wants to play with you and you can't play with everyone at once and that's when you hit them to get them to stop.

Aroldis: Sometimes I want to play alone during choice time. But everyone's bugging me to play with them.

Adult: Ah, sometimes you want to play alone.

Aroldis: Uh-huh.

Adult: Do the other kids know when you want to play alone?

Aroldis: I don't know.

Adult: Do you tell them?

Aroldis: Yes! And I tell them I can't play with everyone at once. But they still don't leave me alone.

Adult: Aroldis, you are doing a very good job of telling me about this. Thank you!

Aroldis: Uh-huh. Are we done yet?

Adult: Well, we could be done if you want us to be done. Do you want us to be done?

Aroldis: Can we talk about it more tomorrow?

Adult: We certainly could.

Next day *(there's no guarantee that you're going to get through all three steps of Plan B in one day; it depends on how long you have and how long each step takes)*:

Adult: Aroldis, remember yesterday we were talking about what makes it hard for you to have a safe body during choice time?

Aroldis: Uh-huh. Are you married?

Adult, smiling: Yes, I'm married. How come?

Aroldis: Just wondering. Do you play any video games?

Adult: I don't play any video games. Are there any you'd recommend?

Aroldis: Minecraft.

Adult: Ah, Minecraft. Yes, I've heard that's a good one.

Aroldis: It's a great one.

Adult: Good to know. So, tell me, do you remember what makes it hard for you to have a safe body during choice time?

Aroldis: Kinda.

Adult: Do you want me to remind you?

Aroldis: Kinda.

Adult: Well, you said that everyone was bugging you to play with them and sometimes you want to play by yourself.

Aroldis: Uh-huh.

Adult: So is there anything else making it hard for you to keep your body safe during choice time?

Aroldis: Not really.

Adult: You sure?

Aroldis: Uh-huh.

Adult: Can I just take a guess about something I was wondering about? *(After you've summarized and asked for more and a kid tells you they have no more concerns, it's OK to check in with the kid if you still have some hypotheses about what's making it hard for them to meet the expectation.)*

Aroldis: Uh-huh.

Adult: Is it ever because there's something you want to play with and someone else is playing with it?

Aroldis, thinking: I don't think so.

Adult: OK, I was just wondering. Sometimes that causes arguments between some of the kids. Not you?

Aroldis: Nope.

Adult: Let me tell you my concern, OK?

Aroldis: OK.

Adult: My concern is that we don't want anyone to get hurt in our classroom because it's supposed to be a safe place for everyone . . .

Aroldis: But they won't stop bugging me!

Adult: Yes, I didn't forget that part . . .

Aroldis: So that's why I hit them.

Adult, moving on to the invitation: I understand. But I'm wondering if there's a way for us to do something about the kids bugging you to play with them and you wanting to play by yourself sometimes and also make sure we're staying safe. Do you have any ideas?

Aroldis, no longer sitting in his chair, and apparently losing interest in the conversation: I . . . don't . . . know . . .

Adult, watching Aroldis wander toward the whiteboard: Aroldis, can you hang in there for one more minute so we can finish our conversation?

Aroldis, now studying some dry erase markers: Can you say it again?

Adult: I wonder if there's a way for us to do something about the kids bugging you to play with them and you wanting to play by yourself sometimes and also make sure we're staying safe.

Aroldis: At home I have a beanbag chair I sit in when I want people to leave me alone.

Adult: Interesting. So sometimes you want to be left alone at home too?

Aroldis: Yeah, like if my brothers and sisters are bugging me.

Adult: Where is the beanbag chair?

Aroldis: In my room.

Adult: And are you thinking we could put a beanbag chair in our classroom and you could go there when you want to play alone or when you want the other kids to stop bugging you?

Aroldis, coming back to his chair: Yuh-huh. And we could tell them that I'm in the beanbag chair I DO NOT want to be disturbed.

Adult: Aroldis, I think that is an excellent solution. And I think it would work. There are some beanbag chairs in the gym. Should I find out if we can borrow one?

Aroldis: Yes! Are we done?

Adult: We are done. *(Normally, the adult would more formally engage the student in pondering whether the solution was truly realistic for both parties and whether the solution truly addressed the concerns of both parties, but their read was that Aroldis was done.)*

. . . .

Difficulties with anxiety, depression, frustration, interactions with peers, family pressures, tough neighborhoods, and any variety of mental health disorders are walking in your door. You're already dealing with those things to one degree or another. Now you have a strategy for learning about and potentially solving those problems.

Non-Talkers

Obviously, the above dialogues involved kids who, with some patience and decent drilling on the part of the adults, participated in Plan B. And they were all able to communicate through the spoken word. What about kids who can talk but, even with patience and decent drilling, don't talk? And the ones who aren't talking because they can't?

Kids Who Can Talk But Aren't: So what if you feel like you've worded the unsolved problem well, you're doing Plan B proactively rather than reactively, you're giving the kid time to think, you've reassured them that there's no rush, and your demeanor and tone are supportive . . . and you still have a kid who isn't taking? Some additional strategies here:

Guess: It's fine to do some hypothesis-testing or some educated guessing.

Use fingers: If the kid isn't responding verbally to your guesses, teach the kid to respond using fingers. Here's the scale:

5 fingers is "Very true"
4 fingers is "Pretty true"
3 fingers is "Sort of true"
2 fingers is "Not very true"
1 finger is "Not true at all"

If five fingers are too many for the student, use three. If three is too many, use the usual two (thumbs-up, thumbs-down). If fingers are not the kid's jam, write "yes" on one sticky pad and "no" on another, place them in front of the student, and have them tap on a sticky pad to let you know if your guess is accurate.

Find another way: If you learn that the student just isn't comfortable expressing their concerns verbally, you could communicate with them by text instead. If they aren't comfortable having face-to-face conversations, you could meet with them via Zoom with cameras off. If you're at a loss, use pictures so the kid can indicate how they prefer to communicate with you.

Kids Who Aren't Talking Because They Can't: Again, a very heterogeneous population. Fortunately, as we've noted, thanks to any variety of assistive technologies, there's never been a better time to try to communicate with nonspeaking kids. But especially in the case of nonspeaking high-support-needs kids, at a very basic level the goal is to help these kids communicate *somehow* (grunting, growling, hand signals) about *something* (preferences, that something is wrong, pain, or a need for sensory input) in some formal way. If we can get the ball rolling with one somehow and one something, we're on our way and can build from there.

By the way, our reference point here is infants. Not because we're equating non-speaking kids with infants, but because infancy is the earliest point at which humans begin to communicate and therefore provides a useful reference point. And because a lot of adults are more empathic toward and curious about infant distress than they are about the distress of kids who are non-speaking, even the empathy and curiosity should be the same. Infants have no words, but they do have unsolved problems and they communicate when those unsolved problems are getting in their way. They aren't able to tell us what's getting in the way, of course, but through our observational skills and guessing we can usually, over time, get a handle on what the different signals mean. Infants also provide us with pretty reliable feedback about whether the solutions being applied to those unsolved problems are getting the job done. We should expect nothing less from a kid of any chronological age or intellectual capacity.

Do these suggestions represent the universe of possible ways to go about helping kids who are significantly compromised in the language-processing realm? Most certainly not. Your creativity, expertise, observational skills, knowledge of a given child, and sense of a child's specific capacities and needs will be crucial.

Q & A

Question: I'm noticing that all these examples involve an individual student and a teacher. Can Plan B be done with an entire classroom?

Answer: Absolutely! Especially on an unsolved problem that affects the entire class. Helping kids solve a problem together—in a way that permits all voices to be heard and respected and leads to a solution that works for everyone—is about as good as it gets. And a great way to foster the kind of climate and culture a lot of educators are trying to create in their classrooms. There's a great video showing what that looks like in the Guided Tour on the Lives in the Balance website. Plan B can also be used on unsolved problems that involve interactions between two kids.

Question: I'm a building principal and I want to move my school in this direction. Am I *mandating* that my staff use this approach or simply *encouraging* it?

Answer: As the building leader, you probably *could* mandate it—there are certainly other things you mandate—but that might not be your best strategy. Better to use your disciplinary data to demonstrate to staff that there are still students you're not serving well, let your staff know that this is a direction you'd like to move in as you feel it's best practice for them and their students, get three or four staff trained up on the ASUP and Plan B, be intentional about making sure that those who are trained help others learn about and practice the model, and create structures that give your staff time to solve problems with their students. And make sure the staff who are struggling are heard, get their concerns addressed, and get the support they need.

Closer Look: Benefit Package

Those three steps of Plan B incorporate the key ingredients required for solving a problem. Because solved problems don't cause concerning behavior—only unsolved problems do—the problem-solving process is also very effective at reducing that behavior. And while those may be the most important facets of what Plan B helps you accomplish, there are additional benefits to solving problems that way.

Plan B also improves communication between kids and their caregivers. Kids who haven't talked in a long time often start talking in the Empathy step of Plan B. As you've read, it could be because you're not trying to talk with them about their concerning behavior anymore, but rather the problems that are causing it. That's huge. And the drilling strategies are really effective at helping kids feel heard, clarify their concerns, feel that their concerns are valid, and keep talking.

Plan B can also improve relationships. The entire dynamic between kid and caregiver changes when the caregiver moves from anger, power, control, and being adversarial to being a curious problem-solving partner. And when adults stop pushing kids to meet expectations in favor of gathering information and working together toward solutions.

Finally, Plan B gives a lot of caregivers and kids something they both badly need in a world that often feels hostile, unkind, insensitive, caustic, and uncaring: human moments. Moments when two people connect, communicate, and work together. Moments when kids feel that you care. Many educators gauge their success by how much their students grow academically. But growth can occur in many different realms, and educators can be facilitators of most of them.

....

"Every day, in a hundred small ways, our children ask, 'Do you hear me? Do you see me? Do I matter?' Their behavior often reflects our response."

—L.R. Knost

9

Agents of Change

To bring what you've been reading to life, we thought you might find it helpful to read a few examples about how the model you're reading about in this book was implemented in various schools and with different kids.

An Educator's Journey

I am a neurodivergent special education teacher, with neurodivergent children of my own. Due to the reality that my own formative schooling was a less than desirable experience, as was that of my own children, I wanted to create a learning environment that would foster a passion for learning within children that would accompany them throughout their life's journey. I sought to engage children regardless of how they were wired neurologically, encompassing all their learning modalities. Based upon the joy experienced by my students, and the feedback I received from paraprofessionals, professionals, and caregivers, I believed that I was well on my way to achieving this goal in my first year as an educator.

Then a six-year-old student named Kiri was placed in my classroom. When seemingly simple requests were made or routine tasks assigned, Kiri would often respond in a defiant manner, which would very quickly escalate to screaming, shrieking, wailing, and crying. These episodes—I suppose we could call them unlucky—would sometimes last more than forty-five minutes and could be heard all the way to the far end of the school. During these incidents, when a staff member would attempt to evacuate the area, Kiri would follow staff and students wherever they went while continuing to scream, shriek, wail, and cry. Due to this, evacuation attempts were stopped. We had ten sets of noise-canceling headphones in our classroom; the first ten students who made it to the bin did all right with Kiri's screaming, the remainder of the students would do their best to cover their ears. Some of them would place their heads on their desks and softly sob to themselves until Kiri eventually calmed.

Daily, Kiri exhibited difficulty meeting social expectations, such as making friends, communicating her basic needs, and responding to other people's needs in socially acceptable ways. In the parlance of the CPS model, the environmental stimuli, academic, and social expectations in my classroom far exceeded Kiri's ability to respond adaptively. Our rewards system didn't work; whenever Kiri missed an opportunity to get an "On-Task Card," she would decompensate, and everyone would suffer. I learned a lot from Kiri.

I had behavioral consultants come in to observe, document, and offer recommendations. Eventually assessments were done. None of which did anything to improve the situation, other than provide more funding for the school and make it possible to get Kiri an educational assistant. We let Kiri draw, because it was something she loved to do. If we didn't disrupt Kiri's drawing, we could get through a relatively peaceful day. For the next few years, Kiri was placed in several different classrooms, but nothing really changed.

Fast-forward to my fifth year of teaching, when I was introduced to CPS. I was inspired by the model, but it took a while for me to fully integrate its practices into my classroom. Still, by spring of that year, the use of seclusion rooms in my classroom greatly subsided and we decommissioned one of these rooms. Problem-solving was now happening daily and some of our highest acuity students were ready to integrate. Then COVID shut everything down.

When we came back from COVID, Kiri was back in my classroom, now with diagnoses of fetal alcohol spectrum disorder; language disorder; specific learning disorder, with impairment in reading; specific learning disorder, with impairment in written expression; specific learning disorder, with impairment in mathematics; attention deficit/hyperactive disorder (ADHD); and disruptive mood dysregulation disorder. She was still wailing, just as she had five years earlier, whenever she was frustrated over an academic or social expectation. Other students avoided Kiri because they didn't like the way she reacted during pretty much every game they played or activity. Furthermore, students were taunting Kiri when she became frustrated. All of this, I learned, had been going on since I'd had Kiri in my class four years earlier. And, still, no one had ever completed an ASUP for Kiri.

So we did that first. Here were some of her unsolved problems:

- Difficulty playing Candy Man (ball tag) with classmate John during lunch recess
- Difficulty printing her letters neatly during our Building Spelling Skills activity
- Difficulty actively participating in our daily numeracy workshop lesson
- Difficulty working on math problems during our numeracy workshops
- Difficulty independently working on her daily math strands
- Difficulty completing her Learn-to-Draw art assignments

We hadn't yet dispensed with our ClassDojo points system that used consequences intended to keep students in line. On the other hand, I and the staff in my classroom had begun solving problems collaboratively with students daily. Kiri was particularly receptive to this.

I began to realize that, so long as I was using adult-imposed consequences, I wasn't truly walking my students through their difficulties, regardless of how much problem-solving we were doing. At the end of winter break, I shared this epiphany with my principal, and he supported me in doing away with the consequences system. He then challenged me to get rid of the last seclusion room in my class. It hadn't been used in a year, but my principal persuaded me that if it was available, it was still a "looming threat." We got rid of it.

Each of the students in my class had a variety of unsolved problems related to difficulties with unstructured times and social interactions; these were addressed through group Plan B meetings. As students began to understand the impact their responses to Kiri were having on her, they started to treat her with more compassion and she in turn became less reactive. We tackled other unsolved problems related to difficulties students were having with substitute teachers, eventually co-creating an "ice breaker" activity that afforded students and substitutes opportunities to get to know each other, while also letting students share their understanding of CPS with the substitutes.

Kiri began to flourish as we solved more problems together. Kiri actively engaged in Plan B meetings and loved solving problems. It turns out that she wanted to connect with people, be heard, and have her feelings validated. As staff solved problems with Kiri, and with other students, Kiri began to connect with her peers in interesting ways. During recess breaks, staff even noted Kiri engaging in activities that weren't of interest to her, because it supported other students. For example, although Kiri wasn't a fan of team sports (she was more inclined toward solitary activities like skipping, somersaulting, etc.), she would frequently cover goal when the other kids in the class were short a goalie for their soccer games. Within our classroom, Kiri would "teach" art lessons to students who were struggling to draw. Kiri began to love school and developed friendships that went beyond the parameters of the school day; she started getting invited to friends' homes for playdates and special events. Kiri transformed from a very reactive state of being (that triggered emotional dysregulation in others) to a place of regulation and reasoning.

It didn't take long for Kiri to reach the point where other students weren't even able to elicit a negative reaction from her. I recall one such occasion vividly. As students returned from an afternoon recess break, Kiri had made it into our classroom ahead of the others and quickly attended to our classroom routines. A peer who was entering the classroom after having "difficulty playing soccer during recess" saw Kiri drawing quietly at her table spot. He proceeded to insult Kiri, saying that her drawings were garbage, that nobody liked them, and other similar things. Keep in mind that Kiri was once the most reactive student I had ever known. Kiri looked at this young fellow and said to him, "You're just saying that because you're upset and trying to hurt me. I'm a wonderful artist, and people like my drawings; even if they don't, it doesn't matter because I love to draw!" It was at that moment that I knew, to the core of my being, that Kiri didn't need to be in my program anymore.

The next year, Kiri was placed in a different special education classroom where CPS was also being used. Kiri would still swing by my classroom periodically to say hi, and to check on her friends.

I often think back to Kiri's journey with fondness now and share aspects of it when training caregivers to problem-solve with the children in their care. I recall one particularly impactful Plan B. Kiri was having difficulty working independently on her daily math strands. Our solution was that she would only work on her daily math strands when I was at school and she could sit at the U-table, close to me; any other time Kiri would work on Zearn math because she knew that she could do that without my help. This solution worked very well, until I was away from school one day. The substitute teacher (I'm sure with the best of intentions) plopped Kiri's daily math strands workbook down in front of her and stated that she wasn't allowed to move on to Zearn math until she had completed four pages of her daily math strands workbook. Kiri tried explaining that she only worked on her daily math strands workbook with me; she even tried showing the teacher the reminder on our math visual that was posted on our classroom whiteboard. Unfortunately, the substitute teacher wasn't receptive to what Kiri had to say. What resulted was Kiri's last massive meltdown. Upon my return to school the following day, I was apprised of what had transpired. We unanimously decided that we needed to create a system to communicate our CPS-informed structures to substitute staff that were not likely to be CPS-informed. After much discussion, we co-created a "Plan C Until We Plan B" bulletin board, complete with visuals of unsolved problems that were on hold for each student. This bulletin board was intended as a large visual that students and staff could reference in situations when students were being told to meet an expectation they weren't able to meet at the given time.

The take-home message? When staff finally took the time to work collaboratively with Kiri to solve the problems that had been impacting her for the duration of her formative education, she flourished. Kiri is not the only student who taught me the importance of challenging the reactive practices that focus on the aftermath of a child's struggles. I now work diligently to see beyond a child's concerning behaviors, looking "upstream" to the expectation(s) that caused them. It may take time to work collaboratively with a child to solve problems, but this is time well spent, as it sets everybody involved up for success. The alternative is wasted time and a lifetime of pain, anguish, trauma, and regrets, and not only for the child.

Another Educator's Story

I'm a former classroom teacher who now serves as a consultant supporting the implementation of CPS in our school board. The *kids do well if they can* mentality was critical for me and my students when I was teaching. Many of the students at my school were living in poverty and were impacted by trauma, and there was a high rate of transience. Many of the students in my classes were achieving well below grade level academically and were struggling with emotion regulation and response inhibition. *Kids do well if they can* reminded me that each child, and each caregiver, was giving me the best that they had every day.

In my grade first/second classroom, students had a wide array of unsolved problems related to general classroom comportment. Many had been part of a kindergarten class the year before that had blazed through five different teachers. By week three in September, we had restructured our entire day! We removed the desks and brought in tables. In our new schedule, we would have about ten minutes of academic activities at a time followed by play-based learning. We were getting about forty-five minutes of formal academics in during the school day. We were able to gradually increase that time, as students gained skills and stamina, and by the end of the school year they had three ten-minute blocks of play per day and the other 270 minutes was learning time.

Early on, I did a lot of Plan C; there were many expectations these kids weren't going to meet anytime soon. While I had spent the summer preparing my program and planning routines, I knew I had to meet the kids where they were at. For example, as a group they had difficulty coming to the carpet, staying at the carpet, and keeping their hands and feet to themselves at the carpet. Edible reinforcement was recommended and, despite my misgivings, I did try. My misgivings were confirmed very quickly. One student would come to the carpet just long enough to get a Skittle, and then she would be gone again. A few others could stay as long as the Skittles supply held out but couldn't focus on learning as they were solely focused on when the next Skittle was coming. The students who were able to stay on the carpet while keeping their hands and feet to themselves didn't need the Skittles. Very quickly it became clear that this problem wasn't going to get solved with Skittles! We shifted to Plan C, eliminating whole group carpet time until we had solved higher priority unsolved problems.

Gym was another difficult time for this group. We had scheduled time in the gym every day and I know the importance of movement during the day. However, two to four students would resist going to the gym, several would be unsafe in the gym, and two to four would have difficulty leaving the gym. We had to handle going to the gym with Plan C. We used this time in the classroom to do Cosmic Yoga or guided visualization. We had a whole-class Plan B conversation about going to the gym. Overwhelmingly, they expressed concerns about the sensory environment there. The space is big, the lights are bright, and most of all the sound echoes. We tried going to gym a few times prepared with headphones and a few books for breaks; one student wore sunglasses. It was still very difficult, so we went back to Plan C. We continued movement breaks in the classroom, including dancing at the carpet with Just Dance videos, exercising on the stage, led by an adult, or taking a walk to the gym, as it was at the far end of the school from our room. We borrowed two sets of pedals for use in the classroom. Lots of problems were solved that year, but the gym expectation was on hold the entire year.

My plans for structuring our literacy block with Daily 5 anchor charts also needed rethinking. Students did not have the skills to be able to read, write, or play letter and word games independently. We had ten iPads, and while most could listen to a story on the RAZ kids program independently, six or seven students would become aggressive when it was time to transition off the technology. We had to adjust our expectations related to reading. Reading could mean looking at the pictures, looking for words you know, or reading with an adult. Over the course of the year, the problems each student was having with reading were solved. It wasn't fast, but development marches at its own pace.

I had lunch with individual students most days. This allowed me time for relationship-building and having conversations with kids. They improved so much in articulating their concerns and coming up with solutions, that twenty minutes was often enough time to solve problems.

We were fortunate to have the support of educational assistants in our classroom. They also had Plan B discussions during the day with individual students as part of our proactive programming plan. Sometimes I used my planning time to have conversations as well. Because the information obtained from students through Plan B conversations was being used to write, teach, and assess IEP expectations, it was essential for planning and therefore a valuable use of my time. Every Plan B conversation reduced the amount of time we spent reacting to behavior.

Students generated wonderful solutions in response to a wide variety of unsolved problems. Jonathan made a card that said "I have something to say" so that when he had his hand up at the carpet, I could take the card and he would know that I saw him and would come back to him, even if another student shared first. Molly agreed to get ready five minutes before her peers when it was time to get ready for recess to reduce the noise and bustle of the coat hooks. Thomas agreed to ask for the pedals to get a movement break on mornings when he arrived at the bell and didn't have time to play outside.

Aiden opted to "pass" every day during our morning circle for the first couple of weeks. In a Plan B conversation, he shared that he needed more time to think. We agreed to leave a copy of the circle prompt on his desk first thing in the morning and an adult helped him record his idea. Gradually he was able to generate and remember his idea on his own. Including the prompt on a slide on the smartboard made this strategy accessible for all.

Shane was having difficulty starting conversations with peers (he was approaching them and yelling in their faces). In the Empathy step, he explained that he was happy to see the person, and he hoped to get their attention so they might hug him. He told me screaming meant that he was happy. Shane articulated that he really likes hugs and that they make his heart not feel sad anymore, and even when he's happy he still loves hugs. My concern was that others feel uncomfortable or scared with his proximity and the yelling. Generating solutions was challenging for Shane. His first, impulsive, suggestion was to hit them. I pointed out that I wouldn't want to hug someone who had just hit me, so this was not realistic or mutually satisfactory. Then he thought maybe if he talked about dogs, they might know he wants a hug. This was not realistic either, as others might not make that connection. We thought about COVID-safe greetings, and wondered about an air hug, but that would not give the physical sensation that he was seeking. At last, he suggested some sensory replacement ideas that he had used last year, using a gym mat or making ground angels. That solution worked for the rest of the year.

Gerald was a student who struggled with frustration tolerance, particularly with academic tasks that he perceived to be difficult, and with conflict over competitive games at recess. Through Plan B conversations he became extremely skilled at articulating his concern and at generating solutions that were realistic and mutually satisfactory. Often, he would request a Plan B conversation, and he began recommending them to other students. He actually posted a sign-up sheet in the hallway outside our classroom door for kids who needed help solving problems. Students added their names and indicated the nature of the problem to be solved.

IEPs were based on our CPS work. Needs were selected from the skills identified on the ASUP. Student concerns collected during Plan B were included as Assessment Data. Recognizing, articulating, and prioritizing one's own concerns; listening to and considering another perspective; and collaborating to generate a solution that is both realistic and mutually satisfactory are all great skills to include as learning expectations.

I have recently transitioned to the role of vice principal and have been implementing CPS in our entire school. I have been able to model the process for teachers when I interact with students in the office. One teacher was openly skeptical about CPS. His student was having difficulty being safe in the gym. During the Empathy step, the student's primary concern was that the teams were not fairly balanced. Partway through the Empathy step, the teacher asked me to stop recording. "His concerns aren't true! I pick the teams based on skill level, so I know they are fair." We talked about perspective and the need to honor the student's perception as the concern was very real in his eyes. In the end, the solution they developed was to select teams together as a class at morning circle so that he could see the process. That solved the problem. I presented at a staff meeting a few weeks later and this teacher stood up partway through to say, "I didn't believe in this, but now I've done it, and I can tell you it works!"

A School's Journey

I'm a school principal. You may be wondering, *How do I begin organizing the effort to implement this change in my school?* Here's a brief description of how I did it.

CPS has been at the heart of my leadership philosophy since 2008. Over the past seventeen years, I've had the opportunity to implement this approach in three different schools, both as an assistant principal and as a principal. While each experience brought meaningful progress, one school stands out as a turning point. It was here that I developed a clear blueprint for successfully introducing and sustaining CPS in a school setting, one that transformed not just discipline practices, but the entire school culture.

The Beginning: Recognizing the Need for Change

In 2007, I stepped into my first leadership role in a public elementary school as an assistant principal at a rural K-8 school. Much of my focus centered on school culture and discipline, and my first year was a whirlwind of learning, along with a steady stream of students being sent to my office. Many were "boomerang" students: those who returned repeatedly throughout the day due to ongoing concerning behaviors in different settings. Each time, I met with them, reviewed expectations, assigned consequences, coached them, and sent them back to class. While some showed improvement, many continued to struggle, making it clear that the traditional approach to discipline wasn't working. I knew there had to be a better way.

That spring, our school social worker attended a training on CPS and recommended that several school staff learn more about it. The *Kids do well if they can* philosophy resonated deeply with me, offering a fresh perspective on how to approach students who were struggling. Plan B provided a structured, systematic way to engage with students in a meaningful and proactive manner. I left the training more than convinced: this was the way forward.

Building the Foundation: Creating an Implementation Plan

Inspired by the training, our team set out to implement CPS in our school. We began with a book study, reading *The Explosive Child*, and experimenting with the model in small-scale applications. Realizing the potential impact, we knew we had to bring this approach to the entire staff.

To ensure successful implementation of the CPS model, we partnered with Lives in the Balance, so we could receive ongoing coaching and guidance. We also established a CPS Implementation Team, which was intentionally composed of representatives from each instructional pod (K-2, 3-4, 5-6, 7-8), as well as special education, guidance, social work, and specials. Our goal was to create a team that reflected a wide range of perspectives, roles, and experiences within the school.

This process included recruiting both formal and informal leaders who had significant influence within the school community, as well as staff members who were initially skeptical of the shift. We recognized the importance of involving individuals with varying viewpoints, as their participation not only provided diverse insights but also helped address concerns and build support across the school. Over time, those who had once questioned the initiative became some of its strongest advocates, demonstrating the power of inclusion and the positive impact of engaging a broad group of school leaders. I learned that someone's initial reaction to CPS is a poor predictor of how they will eventually come to feel about the model. Their involvement was crucial in driving the effort forward and fostering a schoolwide commitment to the CPS approach.

The goal was to create leadership density throughout the school, ensuring that every area of the school had champions of the CPS approach. What is leadership density? As defined by Thomas Sergiovanni, leadership density refers to the widespread distribution of leadership responsibilities across many individuals in a school, rather than being concentrated in a single leader or small group. In this model, leadership is not about positional authority but about shared ownership, collaboration, and collective efficacy. High leadership density ensures that initiatives are sustained and impactful because multiple individuals are invested in their success.

When implementing an initiative in a school—such as a new literacy framework, a social-emotional learning (SEL) program, or a schoolwide approach to supporting behavior—building leadership density is key to ensuring the initiative takes root and thrives. We envisioned each of our subgroups in the school having a leader of CPS who would champion the work for their colleagues.

The first step for our team was to create an implementation plan that would build leadership density as we initiated change. When implementing a schoolwide initiative like CPS, it's essential to consider both technical and adaptive change. Technical change involves the structural and procedural adjustments that provide a foundation for implementation. These are the tangible, logistical elements—such as new policies, training schedules, documentation, and standardized processes—that ensure consistency and accountability. In our CPS rollout, technical changes included integrating the ASUP into student assistant team referrals, adjusting our Response to Intervention (RTI) framework to incorporate CPS, and assigning mentors to support new staff in using the model effectively. These changes were essential in creating a structured system where CPS could be applied across all classrooms and student interactions.

However, true transformation requires more than just updated procedures. Adaptive change focuses on shifting mindsets, beliefs, and behaviors, the cultural elements that define how a school operates. For CPS to take hold, we needed teachers and staff to move away from traditional punitive discipline and embrace the idea that *Kids do well if they can*. This meant rethinking student behavior, developing new habits of problem-solving and collaboration, and creating a shared language around CPS that influenced daily interactions with students. Unlike technical changes, which can be implemented quickly, adaptive change happens gradually as individuals internalize and embrace new ways of thinking and working with students.

Both types of change are critical to success. Technical adjustments provide a necessary framework, but without adaptive change, those structures remain surface-level and unsustainable. Conversely, adaptive change alone—without clear policies and systems—can lead to inconsistency and frustration. By addressing both, we ensured that CPS became not just a program, but a lasting cultural shift in how we support students and approach discipline in our school.

We established the goal of implementing CPS in our school as both an adaptive and technical change, ensuring it was fully in place within two years of the implementation team's initial work. To achieve this, we envisioned our desired outcome and worked backward, developing structured monthly and weekly plans to maintain steady progress toward our goal.

The Implementation Process: Step-by-Step Rollout

Phase 1: Building Knowledge and Confidence (October to March)—School Year One

In Phase 1 of the CPS implementation process, the focus was on building foundational knowledge and confidence within the CPS Implementation Team. During this phase, the team worked to familiarize themselves with the CPS model, refine their understanding of its principles, and gain practical experience in using CPS strategies. The goal was to ensure that each team member felt prepared and supported as they began to apply CPS with students, while also creating a collaborative environment for sharing successes and challenges.

Phase 1 Action Steps:

- CPS Implementation Team engaged in training and coaching.
- Team members read *Lost at School* and reviewed CPS video resources.
- Members practiced CPS strategies with selected students.
- Each member was paired with a "buddy" (cognitive coach) for support and observation.
- Successes were shared in grade-level, team, and staff meetings.

Phase 2: Introducing CPS to the Staff (April to June) —School Year One

In Phase 2 of the CPS implementation process, the focus shifted to introducing the CPS model to the broader staff and ensuring that there was a shared understanding of its importance for student support. During this phase, the team continued to refine their own practice while also preparing the school community for the upcoming implementation of CPS. Key efforts included formal presentations, staff education, and ensuring that leadership demonstrated strong commitment to the initiative.

Phase 2 Action Steps:

- CPS team members continued practicing CPS strategies with students.
- A formal CPS introduction was provided to the staff.
- The presentation was integrated into MTSS discussions, highlighting the need for a structured approach to academic and behavioral intervention.
- Staff were informed that leadership was fully committed to this approach, and the groundwork was laid for full-school implementation.

Phase 3: Full-Scale Implementation (September to December)—School Year Two

In Phase 3 of the CPS implementation process, the focus was on full-scale adoption of the CPS model across the entire school. During this phase, all staff were expected to integrate CPS strategies into their daily practices, using tools like the ASUP to assess and address unsolved problems. The emphasis was on ensuring that the entire school community was actively involved and supported throughout the implementation, with training, coaching, and mentorship to help staff successfully apply CPS strategies.

Phase 3 Action Steps:

- All staff began using the ASUP before making student assistance team referrals.
- Training and coaching were provided by CPS team members.
- CPS "mentors" were assigned to new staff to support their implementation of the approach.

Phase 4: Embedding CPS into School Culture (January to June)—School Year Two

In Phase 4 of the CPS implementation process, the focus was on its sustainability. During this phase, CPS became fully integrated into the school's daily operations, policies, and procedures. The emphasis was on creating consistency across the school, where all staff used common language and processes related to CPS, and Plan B conversations were normalized as part of the school's behavior intervention strategy. Additionally, efforts were made to inform parents and engage them in the process.

Phase 4 Action Steps:

- CPS became an integral part of school policies and procedures.
- All staff used common language and paperwork related to CPS.

- Plan B conversations were normalized as part of behavior intervention.
- CPS was integrated into RTI structures.
- Parents were informed about CPS and its role in our school's behavioral approach.

Managing Complex Change

Implementing a schoolwide initiative like CPS requires careful planning and a deep understanding of how change happens within an organization. One of the most valuable tools we used in this process was the Lippitt-Knoster Model for Managing Complex Change.

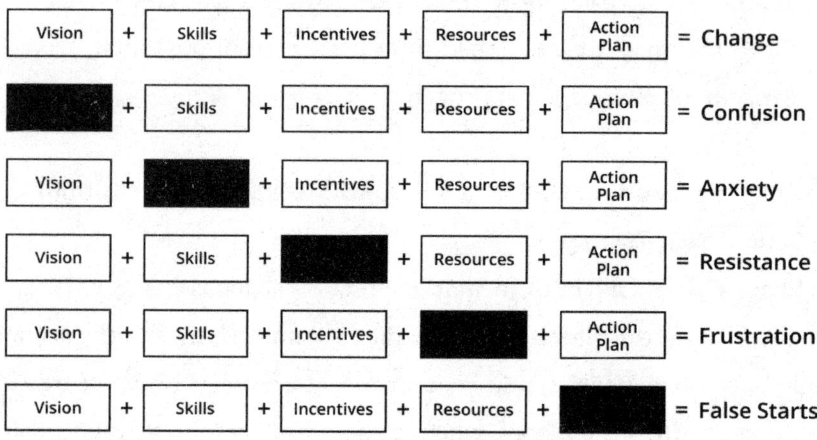

This framework helped us identify potential barriers in our CPS implementation and adjust our approach accordingly. Over the years, this model has remained a go-to reference for me in leading complex changes across various areas of the school.

Knoster's model outlines five key elements necessary for successful change: vision, skills, incentives, resources, and an action plan. If any of these components are missing, teams experience specific challenges, such as confusion, anxiety, resistance, frustration, or false starts. For example:

- **If vision is missing, there is confusion.** Early on, some staff struggled to see how CPS connected to broader school goals. By providing clear messaging on how CPS fit into our MTSS practices and school culture, we helped align everyone with the purpose of the shift.
- **If skills are missing, there is anxiety.** Initially, some teachers felt uneasy about conducting Plan B conversations with students because they lacked confidence in the process. Ongoing coaching, modeling, and peer support helped ease this anxiety and build the necessary skills.
- **If incentives are missing, there is resistance.** Some staff were hesitant to change their approach to discipline. We addressed this by sharing data on office referral reductions, highlighting success stories, and showing how CPS could make their classrooms more manageable.

By regularly referring to Knoster's model, we were able to pinpoint challenges and make adjustments before they derailed the initiative. More importantly, this model has been a valuable tool beyond CPS, helping me to lead other complex changes in our school, whether implementing new instructional strategies, shifting assessment practices, or refining our student support systems. Understanding where a team is stuck is half the battle, and the Lippitt-Knoster model provides a road map to navigate those challenges effectively.

The Results: A Shift in Culture and Discipline

The impact of CPS on our school was profound. Office referrals decreased by 50 percent after full implementation of the model, but the true measure of success went beyond the numbers. The overall climate of the school fundamentally changed; students and staff alike described the environment as calmer, more supportive, and rooted in mutual respect.

Teachers consistently expressed that they felt more equipped to address student challenges before they escalated, using CPS strategies to guide students through problem-solving rather than defaulting to punitive measures. As a result, students responded with greater trust and openness, knowing that their struggles would be met with understanding rather than immediate consequences.

Students too noticed the difference. Many shared that "people are nicer" and that "conflicts are solved more peacefully." They felt heard and respected, which reduced tensions and created a more positive social environment. By prioritizing CPS, students developed stronger conflict-resolution skills, leading to fewer disputes and a more connected school community.

Perhaps most notably, relationships throughout the school deepened. Teachers and students built stronger, more meaningful connections, fostering a sense of belonging and shared responsibility. CPS didn't just change how discipline was handled; it reshaped the culture of the school, creating an environment where students and adults worked together to support growth, learning, and positive relationships.

Lessons Learned: Keys to a Successful CPS Implementation

1. **Start with a Committed Team:** Having a core group of dedicated staff members was essential to leading the charge.
2. **Provide Ongoing Training and Coaching:** Coaching and peer support ensured that implementation was consistent and effective.

3. **Integrate CPS into Existing Structures:** Embedding CPS into MTSS and school policies made it a sustainable part of our framework.
4. **Foster Leadership Density:** Ensuring every grade level and department had CPS champions strengthened schoolwide adoption.
5. **Engage the Entire Staff:** Full-staff training and mentorship were critical in embedding CPS into the school culture.

Moving Forward: Sustaining and Expanding CPS

The work of implementing CPS doesn't stop after the initial training; it requires ongoing practice, reflection, and adaptation to address the evolving needs of both students and staff. By prioritizing proactive problem-solving strategies over reactive discipline, schools can cultivate environments where all students can thrive. In our third year, our focus shifted to how we could more effectively inform and educate all parents about this approach, extending beyond the families of the students we were most directly working with through Plan B.

For any leader looking to implement CPS, the process may seem daunting, but the payoff is well worth it. By taking deliberate steps to build understanding, create buy-in, and integrate CPS into school structures, you can transform the way your school supports students and, ultimately, get the ball rolling toward a more collaborative and proactive educational environment.

....

Whether you and your school are just beginning your journey toward being more responsive to the developmental variability of your students—and changing your practices so they are more collaborative and proactive—or have been moving in that direction already, we look forward to hearing and sharing your stories. Just use the contact form on the Lives in the Balance website. And if you need help, we're happy to assist. Either way, we'd love to hear from you.

Q & A

Question: Thanks for talking a little about the time issue in this chapter. Do you want to say any more about that?

Answer: As we've noted, apparently whoever designed the school schedule didn't account for the fact that academics weren't the only important thing going on in schools and that educators were going to need time to help students who are struggling. Look at the infrastructures we've created in schools to facilitate classroom teachers sending their "problem students" to someone else (the principal, assistant principal, school psychologist, school counselor, school social worker, etc.). Creating an infrastructure to give the folks in the classroom time to solve problems with their students would be easier. So we're going to have to tackle this as a school (by the way, that unsolved problem would be worded as "Difficulty finding the time to solve problems with our students"). And we've seen different schools solve that problem in different ways. Some schools search for "buried" time (before school, after school, during lunch, during recess, during the teacher's prep time, or while the rest of the class is busy working on an assignment). In many classrooms there are at least two adults; one can cover the classroom while the other does Plan B with a particular student. But most schools that have implemented the CPS model have created mechanisms for providing coverage for classroom teachers who want to do Plan B with their students. Often that coverage is provided by principals, assistant principals, school psychologists, school counselors, and school social workers. And classroom teachers are typically delighted to provide coverage for each other. Solving the time problem looks different in every building. But the following is true in every building: solving problems with students takes a lot less time than perpetually dealing with the behaviors that occur when those problems remain unsolved. While we understand the time concern, we find that once schools commit to solving problems with their students, they find and create the time.

Question: I'm a school bus aide. A lot of kids who've had a rough day at school are out of control when they land on the bus at the end of the day. And I know nothing about that rough day. Isn't that the epitome of being late? I wouldn't mind trying to solve problems with these kids, but not if I'm late and not if I don't know anything about what's going on.
Answer: Yes, that's late. And a sign of very poor communication. As we noted earlier, often staff who are spending a lot of time with a student know nothing about their skills and unsolved problems because they've been left out of the discussion. That needs to change. We're glad you're open to solving problems with the kids on your bus, but we need to put you in a position to be able to do it.

Closer Look: The Right Kind of Disproportionality

As is now well known, punitive, exclusionary discipline is disproportionately applied to students with disabilities and those with black and brown skin. That's a very counterproductive, unjust, unacceptable form of disproportionality. But it doesn't mean that all disproportionality is bad.

First, let's establish that there wouldn't be disproportionate application of punitive, exclusionary disciplinary practices if schools weren't using these practices. Those practices are good for no one, irrespective of disability status or skin color.

What's the right kind of disproportionality? Focusing on unsolved problems and solving them. Given developmental variability, some students are going to have more unsolved problems than others. That means it's guaranteed that some students are going to need more problem-solving than others. And that is absolutely fantastic. That's meeting every kid where they're at.

....

"What harms do we accept that we're capable of changing?"

—Dan Heath

10

The Evidence Speaks

As we've noted, schools are big business for many companies, about $100 billion annually in the U.S. alone. Regrettably, schools are not always the most discerning consumers when it comes to what they buy, especially when it comes to interventions for students with concerning behaviors. Interventions that are evidence-based are those that should be implemented with greatest confidence.

One might think that schools would have the leverage to make good choices about the products they purchase. In other words, that schools would be astute customers, with an eye toward proven, evidence-based interventions.

An excellent book, *Investigating School Psychology: Pseudoscience, Fringe Science, and Controversies*, edited by Michael Axelrod and Stephen Hupp, highlights the innumerable school-based interventions for which there is limited or nonexistent evidence of effectiveness, including zero tolerance policies, suicide prevention and intervention practices, prevention programs for risky behaviors, a variety of assessment and instructional practices, and intervention for externalizing and internalizing behaviors.

Practices that aren't mentioned in that book include de-escalating, restraining, and punitive, exclusionary disciplinary practices. These are not evidence-based practices and do not improve safety. Indeed, research shows that those practices do more harm than good.

The fact that these practices have been around for a very long time doesn't mean they make sense. Their continued popularity absent research documenting their effectiveness is troubling. So let's get you up to speed.

An evidence-based practice (EBP) refers to an intervention or practice that has been scientifically tested and shown to be effective for a specific condition or problem. These treatments are supported by rigorous research, such as clinical trials or observational studies, demonstrating that they produce beneficial outcomes for individuals. A treatment becomes evidence-based when it has been consistently supported by multiple high-quality studies that demonstrate its effectiveness and safety. Such studies can include randomized controlled trials (RCTs), which are considered the gold standard, and systematic reviews and meta-analyses, which compile data from multiple individual studies, providing a more comprehensive understanding of the treatment's effectiveness.

As described by the IRIS Center of Peabody College at Vanderbilt University, educators often use the well-established and commonly used practices and strategies that they have seen others use, including their own teachers, never questioning whether these practices are supported by evidence. In fact, some of these practices have been shown to be ineffective or have no data to support them. As stated in IRIS Center documents, "Many schools across the country have adopted zero tolerance policies and associated disciplinary practices for certain behaviors, yet research indicates that these practices are not only ineffective but are also associated with negative student outcomes."

As also noted by the IRIS Center, identifying and selecting an EBP is difficult for education professionals for several reasons:

- There are few opportunities for educators to learn about evidence-based practices (e.g., professional development training, conferences, professional journals, a limited number of websites).
- Specific information about an EBP (e.g., description of the practice, the student population it is effective with, implementation procedures, effectiveness rating) can be difficult to locate.
- EBPs are often presented in formats (e.g., research article) that educators find difficult to understand and, in turn, to apply in the classroom.
- Training on how to read and interpret research findings is often inadequate.
- Written descriptions (especially when composed by vendors) might claim that practices and programs are evidence-based even though they are not backed by rigorous research.
- The criteria for deeming a practice or program "evidence-based" might vary depending on the organization or agency producing the effectiveness rating.
- The term "evidence-based" has not been used consistently. Several similar terms have been used to describe the effectiveness of programs or practices: "research-based," "research-validated," and "best practice." Further complicating matters, these terms have evolved over time and have been used interchangeably; consequently, it can be hard to get past the terminology and determine which practices or programs have been shown by research to be effective.

In other words, there often isn't great clarity about what is meant by "evidence-based," "promising," "research-based," "emerging," "best practice," and "recommended." The first term, "evidence-based practice," refers to a practice with the strongest research evidence. Often, some of the other terms refer to practices that are only backed by anecdotal evidence or professional judgment.

Let's look at some of the practices applied to kids with concerning behaviors in schools. We'll evaluate each based on whether they're early or late, and whether they are evidence-based as defined by demonstrated effectiveness on par with other evidence-based programs or practices in at least two studies, one of which is independent. We'll start with the ones that have a strong emphasis on crisis *management*, which, as you now know, is late.

Crisis Management Emphasis

Nonviolent Crisis Intervention/Crisis Prevention Institute (CPI): CPI offers a variety of programs; its Nonviolent Crisis Intervention Program (NCI) has been providing de-escalation and restraint training in schools and other settings for over forty years. *We were unable to locate any research indicating that such training improves safety or is evidence-based*, so we reached out to the company for clarity and received this response: "We have a library of case studies and customer success stories and of course evidence based references and resources on which our program was based but no published research studies. At this time for public view we do not have any studies that have utilized our program."

Ukeru Behavior Model: Ukeru is an approach to behavior management that emphasizes nonrestrictive techniques for de-escalating and managing challenging behaviors. The model focuses on minimizing the use of physical restraints and seclusion, instead promoting techniques such as redirection, distraction, and positive reinforcement. Ukeru markets and sells blocking equipment that is used to protect both clients and staff against aggressive behaviors. Ukeru encourages caregivers to understand the underlying causes of behaviors and respond with empathy and proactive strategies to address them effectively, accomplished through S.A.F.E.R. principles (*S*ensing the why behind a person's behavior, *A*cknowledging the importance of safety in de-escalation, understanding your *F*eelings, *E*ngaging to praise and build relationships, and *R*eceiving through "Comfort vs. Control"). Comfort vs. Control means "responding to what someone is trying to communicate through nonverbal and verbal cues" and eliminating restraint and seclusion practices. Ukeru also encourages calming strategies such as taking a hot shower, coloring, reading, or eating a snack to help children soothe their fight-or-flight response during times of stress.

Due to the very limited research supporting its efficacy, Ukeru does not qualify as evidence-based. The founder of Ukeru has published two research papers documenting the effectiveness of the model. They are both program evaluations of the sites where Ukeru originated, and they demonstrate a decrease in physical restraints and employee injuries. Several case studies are also available on the Ukeru website.

Low Arousal Approach: The Low Arousal approach is described as a person-centered, nonconfrontational method of managing behavior. It prioritizes behavior management techniques aimed at reducing stress, fear, and frustration to prevent aggression and crisis situations. Caregivers are trained to identify signs of increasing anxiety and intervene to de-escalate situations before problematic behaviors occur. Key components include decreasing demands, avoiding triggers, discouraging nonverbal behaviors that may lead to conflict, and challenging caregiver beliefs about managing challenging behaviors.

The Low Arousal approach does not qualify as evidence-based but is supported by some research that was conducted twenty to thirty years ago. A thorough literature review did not identify more recent studies. This model offered a different approach in a time when behavioral and punitive approaches were by and large the mainstream strategy for working with neurodivergent individuals with concerning behavior. The few studies conducted on the model are more theoretical in nature, with a few quasi-experimental and case studies indicating that Low Arousal approach training increased staff confidence in working with individuals with challenging behaviors.

Safety-Care: Safety-Care, created and provided by the company QBS, is a competency-based "crisis prevention" training program for professionals working with individuals who may exhibit potentially dangerous behaviors. Grounded in Applied Behavior Analysis (ABA) research, it emphasizes positive reinforcement. The training uses behavioral instruction techniques like errorless learning, task analysis, and role-playing to ensure proficiency in essential skills. The model is said to be "progressively restrictive," designed to provide staff with skills for prevention, minimization, and management of dangerous or challenging behaviors, with the option of restraint if deemed necessary. Safety-Care distinguishes itself from other crisis prevention programs through its extensive use of ABA principles. Safety-Care reports that instead of learning to "set limits" or engage in confrontational interactions, Safety-Care trainees are taught to ignore challenging behaviors and concentrate on the individual's strengths and skills. This is achieved through prompting, recognizing, focusing on, shaping, and reinforcing approximations of more desirable behaviors. As noted on the Safety-Care website, "Physical procedures are designed to be both effective and gentle. Each procedure avoids any stress/hyperextension of joints, pain, or skin damage. Holds are used only when there are no other safe choices and only with utmost care for an individual's safety and well-being." Safety-Care is also said to focus on encouraging specialists to understand the effect that past trauma may have on current behavior, within the context of a "whole person" understanding of the individual. Safety-Care's curriculum teaches trainers to identify and help manage triggering events.

We were unable to locate any academic or peer-reviewed published research documenting the effectiveness of Safety-Care. We contacted Safety-Care directly and were told that, in their own research on a pediatric psychiatric hospital, Safety-Care produced a 78 percent reduction in patient injury, a 50 percent reduction in staff injuries, and a 30 percent reduction in restraint and seclusion after two years of implementation. "Beyond that, customers have shared lots of anecdotal data with us showing good outcomes, but that is not published research. Additionally, we have drawn on the ABA and PBIS literature to embed well-evidenced protocols such as differential reinforcement and functional communication training into the curriculum."

Mandt System: With a catchphrase of "supporting people, not just their behaviors," the Mandt System is said to provide training designed to enhance safety by focusing on de-escalation, crisis prevention, and relationship-building. The crisis prevention aspect of the program is aimed at teaching behavior management tools to teachers and students, helping caregivers recognize cues for potentially violent behavior, and promoting desired behaviors. For use in schools, the Mandt System is dedicated to Positive Behavioral Interventions and Supports (PBIS), aiming for full integration of PBIS concepts rather than mere alignment with existing materials. The Mandt System curriculum focuses on how to interact with people who have experienced trauma, including building healthy relationships, healthy communication, healthy conflict resolution, trauma informed services, and implementing PBIS. The Mandt System incorporates restraint in its training, but only as part of a broader strategy and should be used sparingly. "A (restraint) can only temporarily interrupt dangerous behavior, as restraint does not address the root cause of dangerous behavior. The root cause of most dangerous behavior is addressed through meeting people's basic needs and positive behavior supports applied within a trauma informed culture."

Mandt is one of the few crisis management models to provide an honest appraisal of the evidence base for such models and shares the following in their Evidenced-Based Brochure: "To date, we are not aware of any nationally recognized vendor of crisis management training that can claim to be evidence-based using the more traditional scientific definition of evidence-based practice. This is validated by The California Evidence-Based Clearinghouse for Child Welfare (CEBC). The CEBC lists five national crisis management training programs and not one has received a scientific rating. The Mandt System has been utilized in practices that are deemed evidence-based and have contributed to the body of knowledge in the field of restraint reduction."

Therapeutic Crisis Intervention (TCI): Developed by Cornell University in the early 1980s with funding from the National Center on Child Abuse and Neglect, TCI is a model designed for crisis prevention and intervention in residential childcare settings, though its very name betrays its emphasis and explains its placement in this section. This model aids organizations in preventing crises, de-escalating potential crises, managing acute physical behavior, and reducing the risk of injury to both children and staff. It equips child and youth care staff with skills, knowledge, and attitudes to support children during their most challenging times. Additionally, it helps childcare workers understand the significant influence adults have on "children who are troubled" and teaches them to respond sensitively to the emotions and behaviors of youth in crisis. Throughout the process, from prevention to de-escalation to therapeutic crisis management, the program aims to help residential childcare personnel teach children developmentally appropriate and constructive methods for handling frustration, failure, anger, and pain.

The California Clearinghouse includes only one of the studies conducted on TCI in its report of the program, and it was given the classification of

"Not able to be Rated on the CEBC Scientific Rating Scale." This means that currently it does not qualify as an evidence-based practice.

The premise underlying the TCI system is that pain-based and high-risk behaviors can often be prevented by creating a setting in which emotionally competent adults meet children's needs and allow children to heal and thrive through caring and developmental relationships. Developmental relationships are characterized by attachment, reciprocity, progressive complexity, and balance of power. These four criteria work together to help children grow, develop, and thrive. "Children feel safe and learn to regulate their emotions with help from caring adults (co-regulation). When the child is calm, they can discuss the incident with a trustworthy adult and develop better ways to handle stressful situations in the future. Once children are able to manage their emotions, they can negotiate potentially stressful situations occurring throughout the day on their own."

Therapeutic Aggression Control Techniques (TACT2) is a training program focused on trauma-informed approaches to behavior management, de-escalation, and crisis intervention. Established in 1997, TACT2 has been utilized in various settings, including residential treatment facilities, group homes, alternative schools, shelters, and foster care. TACT2 distinguishes between behaviors that are intentional and those caused by emotional problems. "Any staff or parent knows that there are times when children and youth are acting up intentionally. Perhaps they're manipulating adults to get their way, or acting tough to impress their peers, or just messing around because they're bored. We call this Deliberate Misbehavior, grounded in Dr. William Glasser's work on social needs. We teach staff to recognize deliberate cues and to use a corrective approach by setting and enforcing reasonable limits, while encouraging youth to make wise choices before consequences are applied." The key skills taught by TACT2 are active listening for the de-escalation of emotional problems; behavior management skills for deliberate problems; when to and when not to intervene physically; how to protect yourself (using minimum force) if attacked; how to remove a youth from an unsafe area, using teamwork and minimum force; and how to restrain a dangerously unsafe youth, using teamwork and minimum force. TACT2 is not evidence-based and doesn't claim to be.

Schoolwide Emphasis

Next, we describe popular programs that are intended for an entire school. While these programs are not specifically oriented toward crisis management, they are frequently primarily applied to students with concerning behaviors:

Positive Behavioral Interventions and Supports (PBIS): PBIS, also known as PBS in some countries and PB4L in others, derives from the applied behavior analytic (ABA) tradition and consists of a few different components. First, as you've read, it's a three-tiered structure for organizing the supports provided to students. Second (and you've read about this too), it's a set of interventions—such as teaching, reteaching, and reinforcing replacement behaviors and check-in/check-out (CICO)—aimed at preventing unwanted behaviors and promoting positive behaviors. The PBIS framework also emphasizes the collection of behavioral data to make informed decisions about interventions and strategies. In its emphasis on concerning behavior, we view the interventions of PBIS as being late.

The large number of studies documenting the effectiveness of PBIS consist of a mix of academic and behavioral outcomes, a wide array of populations, and a variety of methodologies (randomized controlled trials, quasi-experimental studies, descriptive or correlational studies, single-case studies, case studies, and meta-analyses), many of which do not meet the gold standard of evidence-based practices. Most of these studies have focused on Tier 1 (a more general population of kids) rather than Tiers 2 and 3, have primarily examined the effectiveness of CICO, and haven't typically been focused on kids with significant behavioral issues. As regards CICO, only five of twenty-nine studies met quality indicators to be included as evidence-based practices, and four of those five studies were single-subject designs.

Restorative Practices: Restorative practices (RP)—also known as restorative justice—refers to a set of general practices and beliefs that have been implemented in diverse ways. RP is derived from indigenous conceptions of community justice that are focused on healing rather than punishment. After it gained popularity as a social justice movement in the criminal justice system, schools began to adopt elements of the RP philosophy in education to reduce exclusionary discipline and harsh punitive practices. RP practices can include making amends, healing circles/mediation, and community building exercises. In schools, restorative circles frequently take one of two main forms: community building circles are aimed at fostering strong classroom bonds, while reparative or mediation circles focus on addressing harm that has been caused by concerning behavior, making amends, and creating an agreement for the future. While RP admirably eschews punitive, exclusionary discipline, the aspects of RP that are focused on a student's concerning behavior are late.

RP does not qualify as evidence-based. While schools implementing restorative practices often indicate an important shift in attitudes toward exclusionary discipline—which is a critical first step for reducing disparities based on race and/or neurodivergence—several literature reviews have shown that the evidence base on RP is still quite limited, due both to the types of studies employed and the general lack of impact. In an analysis of seventy-one articles publishing original data on RP between 2000 and 2020,* only four studies used a quasi-experimental or experimental design, which is considered the strongest design for showing the impact of a particular model; more than half of the studies were qualitative. The current available data do not focus on RP's impact on students with significant behavioral needs or cognitive challenges.

The Sanctuary Model: The Sanctuary Model is a framework that promotes trauma-informed care and a culture of safety throughout an organization. Developed by Dr. Sandra L. Bloom, it is grounded in the understanding of trauma's impact on individuals and systems and aims to foster environments where both clients and staff can heal and thrive. The model emphasizes the integration of trauma theory into everyday practices, including the implementation of specific tools and structures known as the Sanctuary Toolkit, which teaches emotional regulation, and use of a shared language, represented by the acronym S.E.L.F., which stands for safety, emotion management, loss, and future. The program is primarily targeted toward individuals experiencing symptoms of PTSD.

Some of the components of the Sanctuary Model are early. The California Evidence-Based Clearinghouse for Child Welfare has rated the Sanctuary Program as a "3," signifying it has promising research evidence in three domains: alternatives to long-term residential care programs, higher levels of placement, and child and adolescent trauma-treatment-system-level programs.

The Boys Town Education Model (BTEM): The Boys Town Model aims to create a positive school climate, reduce disruptive behavior, and improve academic achievement by fostering a supportive and structured learning environment. Key components of the model include

---

* Zakszeski, B., and Rutherford, L. "Mind the Gap: a systematic review of research on restorative practices in schools," *School Psychology Review*, 50(2–3), 371–87.

encouraging and rewarding positive behavior to reinforce good habits and discourage negative ones through positive reinforcement. Social skills instruction is integrated into daily activities to help students develop effective interpersonal skills. Clear and consistent rules and expectations are established across all school environments to provide stability and predictability for students. Immediate and appropriate consequences are applied for both positive and negative behaviors in a timely and fair manner. Data are used to monitor student progress, identify areas of need, and adjust interventions accordingly. Additionally, BTEM encourages ongoing training for educators to effectively implement the model and maintain high standards of practice.

Strategies emphasized in this model include providing social reinforcement, preventing problem behaviors, correcting problem behaviors, teaching social skills, blending social skills instruction and academic lessons, and teaching problem-solving skills. As such, this model is a blend of both early and late interventions.

As explicitly stated by Boys Town, at this time it is not recommended by any clearinghouse of evidence-based models.

Reframing Behavior: In association with the Alliance Against Seclusion and Restraint (AASR), CPI has also developed a new program for schools called Reframing Behavior. Susan Driscoll, president of CPI, has stated that a primary motivation for Reframing Behavior was the recognition that CPI's other programs were mostly geared toward acute moments of crisis. In describing this program, we are, for the moment, putting aside any skepticism and misgivings we might have about a partnership between an organization that purports to advocate against restraint and seclusion and one that continues to train countless educators on how to restrain kids.

Although Reframing Behavior is advertised as a proactive approach, it is heavily focused on understanding the moments when students exhibit dysregulated behavior. The program is centered on four elements:

Reframe Your Relationships is focused on helping educators provide cues of safety and regulation for students. "When we are positive and supportive, our students' mirror neurons cause them to mirror our positive feelings and behaviors." Relationships are built through small, frequent interactions, including greetings, planned touch points, and apologies.

Reframe Your Actions is focused on promoting co-regulation through the relationship between student and teacher, emphasizing the importance of self-regulation for the teacher to promote calmness. This element consists of four tenets: assume stress behavior first, think can't not won't, get curious and ask questions, and change your language.

Reframe Your Awareness is focused on helping educators learn more about themselves and become aware of their own dysregulation. This step promotes awareness of one's body and employing skills to regulate the nervous system.

Reframe Your Perspective, in which educators are taught basics about the nervous system and brain functioning, how behaviors often come from a stress response, how to detect a stress response in a student, and how to know when stress becomes toxic.

We have not seen any research whatsoever regarding the effectiveness of this new program.

Supportable Solutions: Supportable Solutions, a product developed by speech and language pathologist Connie Persike, is said to focus on practical, sustainable strategies for addressing behavioral and communication challenges in educational settings. The model uses The Why Toolkit, which appears to be a conglomeration of many different models and theories, to reframe perceptions of student behaviors. Its assessment tool, Finding The Why, is said to use data-driven analysis and insights from neuroscience to uncover root causes of behaviors, similar to aspects of Functional Behavior Analysis data collection. Its support plan, Beyond The Why, is said to offer trauma-sensitive, neurodiversity-affirming strategies to reduce stress and promote positive behaviors.

On the Supportable Solutions website, the following information is provided: "The Why Toolkit is an Evidence-Based Practice (EBP), as defined by the American Speech-Language-Hearing Association (ASHA). This means it integrates clinical expertise, cutting-edge research, and the perspectives of neurodivergent individuals and their families . . . it was expertly reviewed, piloted by practitioners, and refined with feedback from sensitivity readers." However, because we had difficulty locating any research documenting an evidence base for Supportable Solutions, we contacted the company directly and received the following response: "Supportable Solutions is primarily a business offering practical solutions and support tailored to the needs of educational institutions. While we do not have specific academic papers demonstrating the effectiveness of our services in the traditional sense, we have a track record of successful implementation and positive feedback from schools and educational professionals." Supportable Solutions does not qualify as evidence-based based on the criteria being applied in this chapter.

The Safewards Model: This is a framework designed to improve safety and reduce conflict and containment in psychiatric care settings. Developed by Professor Len Bowers and his team at King's College London, the model identifies key factors and interventions that can create a safer and more therapeutic environment for both patients and staff. The Safewards model proposes ten specific interventions aimed at reducing conflict and containment. These components are heavily weighted toward lateness, with some early components:

1. **Clear Mutual Expectations:** Establishing and communicating clear expectations between staff and patients.
2. **Mutual Help Meetings:** Regular meetings where patients can support each other.
3. **Soft Words:** Using nonconfrontational language and approaches during potential conflicts.
4. **Talk Down:** De-escalation techniques to calm agitated patients.
5. **Positive Words:** Focusing on positive feedback and reinforcing good behavior.
6. **Bad News Mitigation:** Handling the delivery of bad news sensitively to minimize distress.
7. **Know Each Other:** Encouraging staff and patients to learn about each other to build rapport.
8. **Reassurance:** Providing comfort and reassurance to patients, especially during stressful times.
9. **Discharge Messages:** Positive messages from discharged patients to those still in the hospital.
10. **Calm Down Methods:** Providing options for patients to manage their own distress (e.g., comfort boxes).

There is some preliminary evidence suggesting that aspects of Safewards may reduce conflict or challenges that can lead to restraint, but studies on the model have had many limitations (non-experimental, mostly based on literature review) and were inconclusive.

....

And what about the model you've been reading about in this book? The CPS model has been studied primarily in kids with significant behavioral challenges across a wide variety of settings (families, schools, inpatient psychiatric units, and residential and juvenile detention facilities) and is recognized as evidence-based. The accumulated research on CPS—which you can find on the Lives in the Balance website—documents that the model is highly effective at improving kids' behavior (on a par with behavioral interventions), improving adult-child relationships, and dramatically reducing discipline referrals, suspensions, restraints, and seclusions.

Some highlights here: The CPS model was instrumental in helping Fairfax County Public Schools—the largest school system in Virginia—reduce their use of restraint and seclusion from the thousands each year to dozens each year (it helped that they removed the doors from their seclusion rooms!). In a much smaller school system in Maine, restraint and seclusion was being used in only three classrooms but numbered in the hundreds. The CPS model was central to reducing that number to fewer than a dozen per year. In the juvenile detention system in the state of Maine, the CPS model was instrumental in reducing recidivism from 85 percent to 15 percent, and in dramatically reducing the use of restraint and solitary confinement and staff and resident injuries. And in inpatient psychiatry units, several published studies have shown that the model has been associated with dramatic reductions or complete elimination of restraint and seclusion.

Q & A

Question: I work in a special education classroom. It troubles me that so many of the programs we implement aren't evidence-based.

Answer: Us, too. You are, we hope, well-positioned to do something about that.

Question: Why is so much of what we learn about how to handle kids with concerning behaviors oriented toward being late?
Answer: As you know, we have our theories. Human nature. Capitalism. Bad habits. Inertia. All things that can be overcome for the sake of you and the kids.

Question: And there are schools working with kids with concerning behavior that aren't using restraint and seclusion?
Answer: Tons of 'em. Now we need the rest to get on board.

Question: My school has put a lot of effort into being trauma-informed. I'm noticing that that hasn't been a major focal point of this book. Thoughts?
Answer: Well, the CPS model is considered trauma-informed. Which makes sense, since it includes the ingredients of trauma-informed care (emotional and physical safety, collaboration and mutuality, trustworthiness and transparency, and empowerment and choice). That said, in the CPS model, we view trauma as one of many factors that can compromise a kid's ability to handle problems and frustrations. So, while we think trauma-informed care has helped many caregivers be more empathic toward kids with concerning behaviors, and that its emphasis on relationship-building is important, we also know that relationships alone aren't going to solve the problems that are causing a student's concerning behaviors. You need something more. When you're solving problems collaboratively and proactively, relationship-enhancement occurs as part of the process.

Question: Who does the CPS model *not* work for?
Answer: We've heard lots of theories about that. We've heard that it's not for very young kids (that's usually because people haven't checked out the videos in the CPS for Young Kids section on the Lives in the

Balance website). We've heard it's not for nonspeaking kids (you've read about how we approach things with those kids already). We've heard it's not for kids with this diagnosis or that diagnosis (a diagnosis tells you nothing about whether a specific child can participate in Plan B, and even less about a specific kid's skills and unsolved problems). We're having trouble coming up with any "type" of kid who doesn't want to be understood and doesn't want to participate, in whatever way possible, in solving the problems that are affecting their life.

Question: I'm a school system attorney. My job is to keep my school system from getting sued because it didn't respond decisively to a serious concerning behavior. And decisively usually means heavy-duty consequences. Thoughts?
Answer: First, that's an indication of the degree to which consequences have permeated our thinking about effective intervention. Second, what a shame liability concerns would drive your school system to implement a harsher version of what hasn't worked for a student already. Third, consequences are not the only decisive course of action. Plan B is decisive too. And fourth, your best defense is to implement evidence-based interventions. The CPS model is evidence-based.

Question: Do we need parental permission to do the ASUP and Plan B?
Answer: We don't think so, but you'll want to check in with the powers-that-be in your school system to be sure.

Question: I'm a parent. I know this book wasn't written for me exactly, but I want my child's school to use the CPS model. My kid needs it. So far, they aren't listening to me. Advice?
Answer: Identify someone in the building who you think will be sympathetic to your cause. That might be your child's classroom

teacher. It might be the school counselor. It could be the principal or assistant principal. Talk with them. Get the lay of the land. Get their guidance on how you should proceed.

Closer Look: Agenda47

We realize that wading into the political arena is fraught these days. But politicians set the tone and establish policies that affect kids and schools, so their ideas and words matter. And while we're not making a political statement here, we still have faith in the civil exchange of ideas that is integral to the process of solving problems collaboratively. Along those lines, we want to express some concerns about Agenda47, which includes Ten Principles for Great Schools Leading to Great Jobs, as set forth by the Trump administration. Whether or not you are a supporter of the administration, we hope you'll keep reading and take the concerns constructively. And if you've read all the preceding chapters, nothing in this section will come as a surprise.

"Greatness in the classroom requires safety in the classroom." So far so good; but how to get there? "To that end, President Trump will completely overhaul federal standards on school discipline to get out-of-control troublemakers OUT of the classroom and INTO reform schools and corrections facilities, for the good of themselves and their peers alike. This will include supporting immediate expulsion for any student who harms a teacher or another student." The goal of safety is admirable. The method needs some additional thought. We don't have faith that "reform schools" and corrections facilities are going to get the job done. They haven't yet. The answer to helping kids who are struggling is not to demonize them and push them out of the schools that could be helping them but rather to help schools do a better job of meeting these kids where they're at.

"President Trump will end the leftist takeover of school discipline and the juvenile system. He will order the Departments of Justice and Education to overhaul federal standards on disciplining minors to get violent thugs out of our children's classrooms so they can get the professional help they need. When troubled youth are out of control, the consequences must be swift, certain, and strong." As we've discussed, consequences—even if they're swift, certain, and strong—won't solve any of the problems that are causing concerning behaviors. This is worth repeating: *kids with concerning behaviors at school have already been on the receiving end of more consequences than most of us will experience in this lifetime.* If consequences were going to get the job done, they would have worked a long time ago. For most of these kids, the help they need *can* be provided in the classroom. Calling them "thugs" doesn't bring us any closer to helping them and understanding their difficulties. We have not observed a "leftist" takeover of school discipline and the juvenile system. The United States incarcerates more people than any other nation; and we suspend 5 million kids a year, dole out countless dozens of millions of detentions, and (as you've read) still apply corporal punishment in public schools in seventeen of our fifty states. Still plenty of harsh, punitive discipline being doled out, and things are worse.

"President Trump will encourage local school districts to implement a zero-tolerance policy regarding illegal drug use or possession in school with immediate suspension or expulsion." We support realistic efforts to reduce drug use in our kids and in our schools. We are hard-pressed to appreciate how suspension and expulsion will solve this problem. And, as noted earlier, research is quite clear on the fact that the zero tolerance policies that became popularized after Columbine made things worse.

So, while we applaud the emphasis on school safety, demonizing kids and being more punitive isn't going to get us there. Instead—and this is straight from chapter 2—we strongly recommend that we focus on problems rather than the behaviors being caused by those problems, be more collaborative than unilateral, be proactive rather than reactive, accurately interpret concerning behavior, and emphasize developmental variability and expectation management.

Let's get there together. Without politicizing anything, if possible.

....

"Those who cannot remember the past are condemned to repeat it."

—George Santayana

"If compassion and mercy are not compatible with politics,
then something is the matter with politics."

—U.S. President Gerald R. Ford

11

Special Purpose Schools and Restrictive Therapeutic Settings

In a special purpose school, a teacher watches a fourteen-year-old boy, recently expelled from his general education school, punch a hole through a wall after being asked to write an essay. A behavioral interventionist arrives to "de-escalate" him . . . not by addressing the problem that led to his outburst, but by demanding that he sit in a silent reflection room for the rest of the period.

In a psychiatric treatment unit, a twelve-year-old patient who regularly struggles to share during therapy groups becomes dysregulated and starts screaming insults at the staff. It's not the first time this has happened. Instead of proactively trying to understand what was preventing her from participating, the staff physically restrain her (again) while calling for additional backup. She sobs into the linoleum floor, saying "I thought you were supposed to be helping me."

In a juvenile detention center, a fifteen-year-old boy sits in his cell after having spent three days in solitary for participating in a fight during a basketball game. In the absence of a process for solving the problem that caused the conflict during the basketball game, he plots his revenge on his adversary. He knows his plot will likely result in additional charges and increase the amount of time he spends locked up, but he must save face.

What characterizes each of these scenarios?

- The absence of a proactive approach
- A focus on managing and modifying behavior, rather than on solving the problems that are causing them
- The use of power and control rather than collaboration and problem-solving

Where do kids who aren't OK end up if they continue not doing OK? In other words, if their problems remain unidentified and unsolved and if they have unremitting unlucky frustration responses? They go to more restrictive settings, such as special purpose schools, inpatient psychiatric units, so-called boot camps, and residential and juvenile detention facilities. Everything you've read so far is equally applicable to such settings. And often these settings respond with the same approach that has failed these kids already. Even if you don't work in such settings, this chapter has useful information for you.

For many of these kids, the unsolved problems began accumulating quite early in life. In some, the unlucky frustration responses began in infancy; what might have been called difficult temperament. For others, the unsolved problems and frustration responses began piling up as toddlers, when language and locomotion kicked in, giving the kid agency they didn't have before. Regrettably, it is at that exact point in time that caregivers often become obsessed with compliance. That combination of events helps explain why we call it the Terrible Twos. For others, spoken language was slow to or didn't develop, creating a host of problems and frustrations in interacting with the world. Some had a very hard time transitioning from daycare to the increased demands of preschool. Or from preschool to the increased demands of kindergarten, or from kindergarten to the increased demands of grade school. All points in development—we might call them *points of vulnerability*—where expectations can exceed a child's capacity to deliver the goods.

Others didn't read or write or develop social skills on a pace with expectations. (It doesn't help that we're placing those expectations on kids earlier in development. Of course, as we've noted, the earlier in development we place expectations on kids, the more likely those most vulnerable are to struggle.) Some had difficulty with hyperactivity and/or poor impulse control and/or focused attention, which made it hard for them to meet increasing demands for these skills at school.

The bottom line is that if problems aren't identified and solved (the earlier the better) they get worse and continue to accumulate. And if caregivers are of the belief that behavior charts, loss of privileges, detentions, suspensions, expulsion, and hitting are going to solve those problems, things will get even worse, and kids will be pushed toward alienation and disenfranchisement. For those who still think these kids just need a good kick in the pants—"tough love," perhaps—let there be no doubt: these are the most overcorrected, overdirected, overpunished kids in our society. In other words, been there, done that.

So, it shouldn't come as a surprise that, at some point along the way, there's a good chance these kids will start becoming more anxious and depressed, stop showing up at school, become suicidal, or exhibit frustration responses that are increasingly unlucky. Nor is it surprising that those kids often find their way into a special purpose school, an inpatient psychiatry unit, or a residential or juvenile detention facility. All quite late. And quite expensive. Regrettably, many function as containment zones or stabilization holding pens. The applicability of what you've read so far will mostly be affected by the usual length of stay in your facility.

In such facilities, the developmental variability is striking, and meeting kids where they're at is even more critical. After all, these facilities are at, or close to, the so-called end of the line. They often represent our last best chance at focusing on skills and unsolved problems and giving kids agency in solving those problems.

In facilities such as inpatient psychiatry units and short-stay juvenile detention facilities, the average length of stay is three to ten days. What can be accomplished in such a short time?

Not a whole lot. Let's first talk about what can't be accomplished in three to ten days. Staff in inpatient units often feel pressure to get a kid looking really good in the three- to ten-day window, or to compensate for what they believe is incompetent parenting. Sounds to us like a recipe for trying too hard. And trying too hard often comes in the form of placing expectations on kids that they can't meet and the use of some form of behavior modification system to incentivize compliance. So, when kids communicate that they're having difficulty meeting those expectations through their concerning behavior, there's an excellent likelihood they will be greeted with punitive discipline and restraint and seclusion.

We've heard it said that differential diagnosing is facilitated by placing expectations on kids that cause them to become frustrated so the "diagnosers" can see the kids at their worst. Ludicrous. We've established that a diagnosis isn't going to tell us very much about a kid, so getting the diagnosis right definitely shouldn't be the primary goal of an inpatient stay. If you want to know what a kid's frustration responses are, and what unsolved problems set those frustration responses in motion, ask their caregivers (before they step foot on the unit). Moreover, a significant percentage of kids in inpatient units and juvey facilities have trauma histories. A milieu that emphasizes power in the service of compliance is the exact opposite of what they need. It's also hard to conduct a good medication evaluation in under ten days.

Many medications that are prescribed for High Acuity kids just don't work that fast.

So, the best use of that timeframe is temporary stabilization and a high-quality assessment, starting, preferably before the kid even walks in the door, with the ASUP. The biggest favor an inpatient unit or short-term juvey facility can do a kid is to be the place where, finally, their skills and unsolved problems are identified. As you've already read, it's a pretty surefire bet that's never been done.

Do the ASUP before the kid walks in the door? Of course. If the ASUP isn't done before the kid arrives, then staff have no knowledge whatsoever of what sets the kid off, and that sets the stage for surprises, which are late. No staff member relishes surprises.

The ASUP isn't the only assessment tool available to staff in short-stay facilities. There's also Plan B. Even in three to ten days, staff can begin the process of proactively gathering information from kids about what's making it hard for them to meet the expectations that are causing the concerning behaviors that prompted the inpatient admission in the first place or that are causing the kid to balk at the expectations of the unit. It might not be possible to solve many problems in such a short time, but the information gathered will be very useful to whoever gets the kid next. If—as in the case of kids who end up "stuck" in inpatient units—the stay is longer than ten days, it might be more feasible to get some problems solved; it might even be possible to involve family members in those Plan B discussions.

So, if a kid is, for example, refusing to participate in art therapy on an inpatient unit, there are two potential ways for staff to respond:

"That's what we're doing right now. You need to go to art therapy now." That's the power-and-control approach, and the only assessment information you're going to obtain from that approach is a fresh reminder of how the kid responds when they're frustrated.

"Ah, you're having difficulty going to art therapy. You don't have to go to art therapy. But I sure would be interested in knowing what's making it hard for you to do that." That's the collaborative, information-gathering approach. And if the kid has had difficulty going to art therapy previously (in other words, this isn't the first time), that conversation should take place proactively. Unsolved problems are an assessment opportunity; an opportunity to gather information, not an opportunity to use whatever means is necessary to enforce compliance.

What do staff do during shifts? They do Plan B with kids. They don't wait until kids spin out of control before leaping into action. What's talked about at meetings during shift changes? The problems that need to be solved during the next shift and who's solving them. They don't wait for those problems to "pop up" before they try to solve them.

Ultimately, the inpatient unit's discharge summary is evidence of whether the admission was useful, helpful, and worth the money. If the discharge summary provides yet another lengthy description of all the bad things that have happened in a kid's life, or yet another spin on the diagnoses that summarize the kid's concerning behavior, count us out. Just like a good FBA, the discharge summary should provide a description of the skills that are making it hard for a kid to respond adaptively to problems and frustrations—that information alone could have a big impact on the lenses of those reading the discharge summary—and a comprehensive list of the unsolved problems that need to be solved once the kid is discharged.

Special Purpose Schools, Residential Facilities, "Boot Camps," and Long-Term Juvenile Detention Facilities

As you've read, what distinguishes these facilities from those we discussed in the above section is length of stay. You still want to start with everything we recommended for short-stay facilities, but because you have the kids longer, you're also on the hook for solving problems. Lots of them. In this respect, these settings don't differ greatly from the typical special education classroom. And the problem-solving doesn't look any different from the examples you've already read or seen.

One critical focal point in these environments is staff safety. In some psychiatric and residential facilities, employees have the legal right to refuse to work if they feel unsafe. If multiple staff members refuse to work due to safety concerns, workers' unions and regulatory agencies need to conduct investigations (unions are not insignificant in many school systems as well). When these refusals are attributed to a widespread feeling of insecurity, the employer is legally obligated to provide additional training and resources to staff.

Regrettably, the training is often in the form of crisis-management. This means that rather than investing in proactive, collaborative, relationship-based interventions, many facilities continue to emphasize restraint training and behavioral control techniques that reinforce a culture of containment rather than therapeutic rehabilitation.

Administrators, including psychiatrists and facility managers, frequently find themselves in a difficult position. On one hand, they recognize that certain restraint and isolation measures are counterproductive and do not align with best clinical practice. On the other hand, they fear that reducing these measures will lead to an increase in staff refusals to work, triggering labor disputes and investigations. This tension results in a system where restrictive interventions persist, not because they are effective but because they are seen as the only way to manage staff safety and legal liability.

Because staff are primarily being trained on what to do when kids are already escalated, they often feel powerless and fearful. In the absence of proactive options, their survival instincts kick in, fueling an overreliance on restraint and isolation.

"If we were better equipped to manage risk, we wouldn't need to use these methods as often."

"We're told to focus on behavior, but we know these kids need more than that. They need real support, not just consequences."

Late interventions in these settings fall into two categories:

- **Planned Measures:** These are preapproved strategies for managing a patient's recurring challenging behaviors. If a patient exhibits consistent patterns of distress (e.g., aggression, self-injury), a structured intervention plan is developed to outline when and how measures like containment or isolation should be used. The "planned" part can be deceptive, since it infers that an intervention is early. But not if all we're planning is to be late.
- **Emergency Measures:** When a patient poses an immediate danger to themselves or others, emergency measures are implemented. These include physical restraint, forced isolation, and chemical sedation. In general, such interventions are only necessary because of the failure to be proactive; thus, they fail to address the underlying distress that triggered the crisis in the first place.

When an intervention escalates to the point where restraint, seclusion, or forced removal become necessary, a review process is triggered. Often a multidisciplinary team—including psychiatrists, nurses, educators, and security personnel—evaluate the incident. Their goal is to analyze how the intervention was handled, whether alternative de-escalation strategies were attempted, and what systemic adjustments could reduce the likelihood of similar events in the future.

However, this process often focuses on what happened *once a kid became escalated*. Often the process doesn't focus on what caused the kid to become escalated and how it might have been possible to keep them from becoming escalated in the first place. Moreover—here it comes again—the process typically takes place with little to no input from the patient themselves. Worse still, while the team is multidisciplinary, all members come from within the institution itself, having been trained in the same methodologies and using the same analytical tools. This homogeneity in perspective tends to reinforce existing intervention patterns, leading to the same outcomes time and time again.

....

As a recap, here are the components involved in transforming these and shorter-stay facilities from reactive containment to proactive intervention. Several key changes are necessary:

- **Completion of the ASUP Before Admission:** The information that is gathered is provided by previous caregivers or professionals who interacted with the child. Their insights about the specific unsolved problems and frustration responses that led to the child's placement can serve as a foundation for crisis prevention.
- **Implementation of Proactive Strategies from Day One:** Once the ASUP is completed, the assessment continues, with staff immediately beginning the process of gathering information from the resident about expectations they're having difficulty meeting—attending school, taking medication, or staying safe in their room—rather than waiting for issues to arise.
- **Rapid Prioritizing and Expectation Management:** There is no need to observe a child for weeks before identifying and solving problems, as is the case in some institutions. With the ASUP in place, problem-solving can begin immediately. And since these are High Acuity kids—they have a lot of unsolved

problems—it won't be possible to solve all of them at once. As such, Plan C is a big deal in such facilities as well. It's critical that staff are clear about what problems are and aren't being solved for each kid.

- **Redefining Mission:** If the mission of the facility is unclear, there is no job description. If there's no job description, there is no shared mentality or set of practices that govern how staff should interact with kids in their care. Not good. At all. Here's a sample mission statement for restrictive therapeutic facilities (it's not radically different from the mission statement for schools that appeared in chapter 6):

  We strive to provide an environment in which kids in our care feel safe and understood, and where we meet each kid where they're at. We place a very strong emphasis on crisis prevention, meaning we identify the expectations kids are having difficulty meeting prior to admission and begin gathering information from kids about what's making it hard for them to meet those expectations as rapidly as possible. If length of stay permits, we solve those problems collaboratively and proactively. We eschew the use of power and control methodologies and motivational procedures that have the potential to cause these kids to escalate. We employ strategies that are nonpunitive and relationship- and skill-enhancing. We also strive to pass along what we've learned about each kid to those who will be caring for them after their stay, and further strive to ensure that, upon discharge, they are placed in settings that are similarly nonpunitive, collaborative, and proactive.

- **Redefining Staff Training and Support:** Training should provide staff with the knowledge and skills to implement the mission. While it is important for staff to have the skills to deal with extreme circumstances, they should be trained in identifying problems and solving them collaboratively and proactively to dramatically reduce the likelihood of those circumstances. Line staff are not treated as baby-sitters; they are trained to be a critical, indispensable aspect of information-gathering and treatment.

Q & A

Question: I work as line staff on a short-term inpatient unit. You're right, I hate surprises. I also hate restraining and secluding kids. I don't love being characterized as a baby-sitter, but there's something to that. I always thought there could be more to the job than being the person who leaps into action once a kid is already upset, but I wasn't sure what that could look like. Thanks for the road map. Now, how do I get my unit to do this?
Answer: Sure thing. Maybe the first best step is to get the good folks who run your unit to read this book.

Question: I also work as line staff on an inpatient unit. We've received a lot of training on trauma-informed care and relationship-building, and I feel that such training has helped me be more empathic to the kids on my unit. But now I understand that while relationship-building is a good thing, it's not sufficient. How can we possibly be trauma-informed if we're still restraining and secluding kids?
Answer: Restraint and seclusion are utterly incongruent with trauma-informed practices. But in many trauma-informed programs, relationship-building is really all staff are being trained on. And you're right: as we've noted, while relationship-building is a big deal, if that's our only active treatment ingredient, we're not solving any of the problems that are causing a kid's frustration responses. It's not enough.

Question: Do I need to build a relationship with a kid before I can do Plan B with them?
Answer: Plan B is going to build the relationship for you.

Question: I work in a juvenile detention facility. A lot of the kids I work with have broken the law. Don't you think it's important for them to know that there are rules that need to be followed, no questions asked?
Answer: It's important for them to know that there are rules that need to be followed, though we'd prefer to call them expectations. They're locked up because they're having difficulty meeting those expectations. So, you have a lot of questions to ask, especially about what's making that hard for them. They weren't born breaking the law. That said, as you've read, some have been on a path of failure for a very long time, have been on the receiving end of inestimable amounts of punishment, and lost faith in the adult species a long time ago. Identify their unsolved problems. Solve those problems collaboratively and proactively. Listen to them. Find out what's getting in their way. Restore their faith. Give them hope.

Question: I too work in a juvenile detention facility. I hear all kinds of labels applied to our residents: conduct disorder, sociopath, psychopath. Safe to assume you're not real keen on these characterizations?
Answer: Very safe. Those labels—just like attention-seeking, manipulative, coercive, unmotivated, and limit-testing—don't tell us anything about a kid's skills and unsolved problems, aren't actionable, and don't tell us what we should be talking with kids about during shifts. They make it sound like a kid "has" something. Long ago, a psychiatrist name Thomas Szasz referred to what was then called

"mental illness" as "problems in living." That's a more apt description of what they "have," and if we're using the ASUP to identify those unsolved problems, we can start solving them collaboratively and proactively.

....

"Every system is perfectly designed to get the results it gets."
—William Edwards Deming

12

Be Bold

We began this book by highlighting the compelling signs that tell us that all is not well with many kids. We also reviewed the myriad changes that have occurred over the past two decades that have made it harder to be a kid. And we established that a lot of those changes are things educators can't do anything about. That doesn't mean educators can't do anything, it just means there are many things you can't do anything about. What you can do—in the six hours a day, five days a week, nine months a year that a kid is in your care—is create a school and classroom ecosystem, climate, and culture that takes into account the reality that more students than ever are struggling, hurting, and vulnerable. And we described the changes we've seen move things in that direction in many schools.

You can't do that much about social media use outside of school, though you can, as some schools have done, galvanize kids to address the issue collectively. While you could unilaterally ban cell phones in schools, as some states have done, you could also engage kids in the process of solving the problem of cell phone use in schools.

You can't do much about cyberbullying and the exposure to idealized images kids are subjected to online, but you can create an ecosystem in which individual differences and developmental variability are acknowledged and celebrated.

You can't do anything about the pressure to excel placed on kids these days by parents and legislators and society, but you can create an ecosystem where you're meeting every kid where they're at.

You can't do anything about what's going on in a student's family, but you can create an ecosystem in which kids are heard, have agency, and are engaged in solving the problems that are affecting them at school.

You can't do much about the social isolation and loneliness many students feel outside of school, but you can do something to help them feel a sense of belonging and connection at school.

You can't do anything about the ostracization, discrimination, and lack of support many kids may experience outside of school, but you can make sure they don't experience those things while they're inside your school.

You can't do anything about traumas the kids have experienced outside of school, but you can create a supportive, protective ecosystem that reduces the likelihood of them being traumatized while they're inside your school.

You can't do anything about helicopter parenting, but you can give kids agency and help them feel that they are active participants in solving problems at school.

You can't do anything about factors outside of school that are making it hard for students to attend, but you can make sure the curriculum is meaningful and connected to their lives and that they feel seen and valued when they do show up.

If you do what you *can* do, you'll enhance the mental health of your students, decrease the likelihood of concerning behavior, give them the support and hope they need, give them a sense of belonging, and create a culture and climate that encourages kids to show up instead of staying away. It would be great if your entire building moved in this direction. But always remember that often it is one educator who affects the trajectory of a student's life.

My colleagues in the Athol-Royalston Regional School District in Massachusetts have put a great deal of effort and thought into a vision for graduates. Here's what they're aiming for:

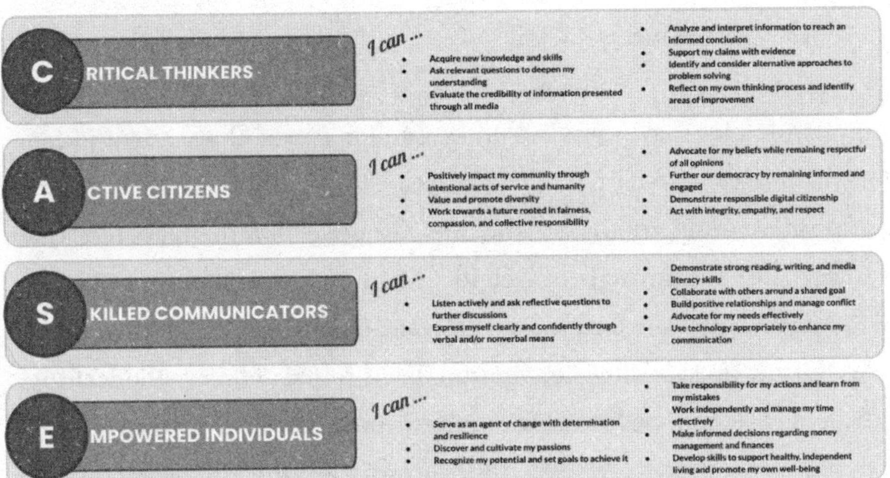

As you can see, a lot of the outcomes they're trying to achieve aren't related to academics. And a lot of those outcomes would be fostered by solving problems collaboratively and proactively with their students.

In other words, there are lots of things your students could say when they're reflecting on the role you played in their lives, many unrelated to academics:

"She taught me how to graph sine and cosine waves."
"He believed in me."
"They helped me overcome my shyness."
"She listened to me."
"He helped me get through a tough time in my life."
"They understood me."

"They made me feel important."

"They saw me."

"She liked me at a time when I was having trouble liking myself."

"They heard me."

Academics may not wind up as a major aspect of a student's identity. But that doesn't mean you can't help them find an identity that is positive and productive and sets the stage for them to feel that society has a meaningful place for them.

We've questioned a lot of conventional wisdom in this book. We think questioning conventional wisdom is a very good thing. If conventional wisdom and standard practice were getting the job done, we wouldn't see so many educators leaving the profession, so many kids struggling, so many concerning behaviors, and so many detentions, suspensions, expulsions, uses of corporal punishment, restraints, and seclusions.

The changes we've described are going to look different in every school. Every school system, school, and classroom is different, and they all operate under different pressures, policies, politics, hierarchies, and socioeconomic circumstances. Our goal in writing this book was to get the conversation going and set forth some ideas, knowing full well that you'd need to tailor things to your specific circumstances.

Here's how you'll know you're getting there:

- All staff understand that concerning behavior is a frustration response . . . and that the nature of a student's distress response relates to skills rather than motivation.

- All staff understand that frustration or distress responses occur when kids are having difficulty meeting specific expectations.
- Your school has made the massive shift from focusing on concerning behavior (and modifying it) to the problems that are causing those behaviors (and solving them).
- The ASUP is being used to proactively identify unsolved problems for your High Acuity kids.
- Plan B is being used to solve some of those problems; Plan C is being used to prioritize, stabilize, and/or manage expectations.
- You have staff in your building who are coaching others along in using Plan B.
- All the above are clearly explicated in your expectations for staff; it's in the job description.

We need to be responsive to what's walking in the door. We need to meet kids where they're at. We need to be solving problems with kids instead of modifying their frustration responses. We need to be collaborative, not unilateral, in solving problems. We need to be consumed with being early. And we need to take a hard look at structures that are making those things hard and change the things that need changing. How all of that translates to your situation is up to you.

Why not just stick with things as they are and see if things go better? Because things haven't been going better for a lot of kids for a long time. And things can't stay the way they are now.

So we need to be bold. Now. It's your classroom. It's your building. Yes, the odds have been stacked against you. But your students are counting on you. So is society.

Let's do this.

....

"The enemy of the conventional wisdom is not ideas but the march of events."

—John Kenneth Galbraith

"I hope that someday we will learn the terrible cost we all pay when we ignore or mismanage those people in society who most need our help."

—The Hon. Judge Sandra Hamilton, Provincial Court of Alberta, Canada

"There are those that look at things the way they are, and ask why? I dream of things that never were, and ask why not?"

—George Bernard Shaw

Acknowledgments

Many people were central to the development of this book as both readers and thought partners. We are grateful to Nina D'Aran, Amy Hall, and Marsene Caswell for helping us think through many of the issues we raise. We also want to recognize Anna Cait Wade for the outstanding research she did on the various models of care described in Chapter 10. Thanks also to Kelly McGowan, Hamish Allan-Caney, Cynthia Greene, Torrie Nightingale, Karin Ney, Laura Murray, Jenny Hunt, and Jenny McBrady for providing insightful and helpful feedback.

We especially want to acknowledge the countless thousands of educators we have worked and collaborated with over the past three decades. You have taught us a lot. We know how passionate you are about your work and how much you care about kids; admire how you maintain hope and energy despite the initiatives, politics, and societal crosswinds that make your jobs more difficult; know you lose sleep over students who are struggling; and recognize that you do the best you can under often-impossible circumstances. This book is for you, and we sincerely hope you find inspiration, hope, and solutions in its pages.

Index